Elite • 223

The Etruscans
9th–2nd Centuries BC

**RAFFAELE D'AMATO
& ANDREA SALIMBETI**

ILLUSTRATED BY GIUSEPPE RAVA
Series editor Martin Windrow

OSPREY PUBLISHING
Bloomsbury Publishing Plc
Kemp House, Chawley Park, Cumnor Hill, Oxford OX2 9PH, UK
1385 Broadway, 5th Floor, New York, NY 10018, USA
29 Earlsfort Terrace, Dublin 2, Ireland
Email: info@ospreypublishing.com

OSPREY is a trademark of Osprey Publishing Ltd

First published in Great Britain in 2018

A catalogue record for this book is available from the British Library

ISBN: PB: 9781472828316; eBook: 9781472828309; ePDF: 9781472828323;
XML: 9781472828330

22 23 24 25   10 9 8 7 6 5 4 3

Editor: Martin Windrow
Index by Alan Rutter
Typeset by PDQ Digital Media Solutions, Bungay, UK
Printed and bound in India by Replika Press Private Ltd.

EDITOR'S NOTE

In the body text, most sites of archaeological finds are given with their
modern place names preceding their ancient names, e.g. Narce/*Tevnalthia*.

ARTIST'S NOTE

Readers may care to note that the original paintings from which the colour
plates in this book were prepared are available for private sale. All
reproduction copyright whatsoever is retained by the publisher. All
enquiries should be addressed to:

Giuseppe Rava, via Borgotto 17, 48018 Faenza (RA), Italy
pitturediguerra@libero.it

The publishers regret that they can enter into no correspondence upon
this matter.

Osprey Publishing supports the Woodland Trust, the UK's leading woodland
conservation charity. Between 2014 and 2018 our donations were spent
on their Centenary Woods project in the UK.

To find out more about our authors and books, visit
www.ospreypublishing.com. Here you will find extracts, author
interviews, details of forthcoming events, and the option to sign up for
our newsletter.

DEDICATION

To the late Gabriele Cateni, the last of the Etruscans

AUTHORS' ACKNOWLEDGEMENTS

The authors would like to express their gratitude to all the scholars, friends
and colleagues who supported this project. First of all, to Dr Marina Mattei,
curator of the Capitolini Musei, Rome, who assisted us during trips to the
capital and South Etruria, and in locating material in Roman and Tuscan
museums; and to Prof Livio Zerbini of Ferrara University, for his valuable
help in obtaining permissions for access and photography.

Our thanks also to three eminent scholars: to Dr Prof Mario Iozzo, current
director of the Archaeological Museum of Florence, who opened the
Museum's treasures for us, including the reserve collection; to Dr Cianferoni
Giuseppina Carlotta of the Soprintendenza per I Beni Archeologici della
Toscana, former director of the Museum, for access to the 'Amazons
Sarcophagus'; and, last but not least, to our dear friend Gabriele Cateni,
who gave us photographic access to the Museum Guarnacci in Volterra,
just a year before God called him to a better life.

For assistance in the field we are indebted to Dr Massimo Bizzarri, who
joined us in many of the Etruscan localities, and to Dr Andrey Negin, to
whom we also owe some of the illustrations. Particular thanks also to Dr
Maurizio Martinelli, for providing a copy of his important work on
Villanovan armament.

Photographic credits are owed to the following museums and institutions
(pictures marked 'author's photo' were taken by Raffaele D'Amato):
Archaeological Museum of Ancient Olympia; National Archaeological
Museum, Tarquinia; Etruscan Museum Guarnacci, Volterra; National
Archaeological Museum of Umbria, Perugia; Museum of the Etruscan
Academy and city of Cortona; National Archaeological Museum, Florence;
National Archaeological Museum Gaius Cilnius Mecenas, Arezzo; National
Archaeological Museum, Chiusi; the Soprintendenza Archeologica del
Lazio e dell'Etruria Meridionale; Museum of Antiquities, Turin; National
Archaeological Museum, Siena; the Vatican Gregorian Etruscan Museum;
British Museum; Ure Museum of Greek Archaeology, University of Reading;
Whiteknights.

As always, we are deeply grateful to the *magister* Giuseppe Rava, for
exercising his usual skill to bring the ancient Etruscans back to life.

CONTENTS

THE ETRUSCANS
9th–2nd CENTURIES BC

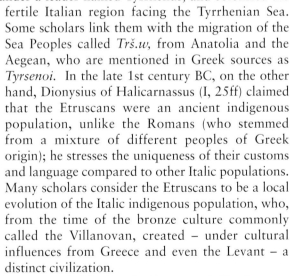

HISTORICAL INTRODUCTION

Etruscan lord or *dynotatos*, as depicted on the 4th-century BC 'Amazons Sarcophagus' from Tarquinia – ancient *Tarchuna*. He wears a Pseudo-Corinthian helmet, and a *linothorax* linen corselet apparently with metal reinforcement on the shoulder-guards. He wields a spear and a *hôplon* shield; note also the sword hilt, and (left of it) the artist's detailing of the fastening up the left side of the corselet. (Archaeological Museum, Florence; author's photo, courtesy of the Museum)

Dazzled by Imperial Rome, we may often forget its deep roots in the Etruscan world. The *Rasenna*, as they called themselves, were the most brilliant culture of North-Central Italy in the 1st millenium BC; their civilization extended from the Po Valley down to the boundaries of ancient Latium, especially between the 7th and 5th centuries BC. From the outset, Etruscan culture appears to have been distinct both from that of the contemporary Greek diaspora – by which it was, nevertheless, deeply influenced – and also from that of the Romans, though they in turn absorbed much from the people they called the *Tusci*.

The origins of the Etruscan peoples are still debatable. According to Herodotus (I, 94) and Hellanicus (*Dionysius*, I, 28), they came from Lydia in Eastern Asia Minor, under a leader named Tyrrhenus, and colonized the fertile Italian region facing the Tyrrhenian Sea. Some scholars link them with the migration of the Sea Peoples called *Trš.w*, from Anatolia and the Aegean, who are mentioned in Greek sources as *Tyrsenoi*. In the late 1st century BC, on the other hand, Dionysius of Halicarnassus (I, 25ff) claimed that the Etruscans were an ancient indigenous population, unlike the Romans (who stemmed from a mixture of different peoples of Greek origin); he stresses the uniqueness of their customs and language compared to other Italic populations. Many scholars consider the Etruscans to be a local evolution of the Italic indigenous population, who, from the time of the bronze culture commonly called the Villanovan, created – under cultural influences from Greece and even the Levant – a distinct civilization.

It is probable that the Etruscan civilization was an exceptional blend of cultural influences from outside (the Mediterranean and Central Europe) with a local ethnic group, invigorated by the influx of several minorities from the Aegean Sea and Asia Minor. According to tradition (Strabo, V, 519; Cato, Fr. 45 P; Lycophr., *Alex.* 1248–1249 *cum scolio*), the origin of the Etruscan entity should be ascribed to Tarchon, identified with Tyrrhenus, and therefore to the city of *Tarch(u)na* (Tarquinia), considered by Verrius Flaccus (*Res Etruscae* fragment 1P) to be the original of what became the 12 Etruscan cities of the so-called *Dodecapolis*. The historical memory of consanguinity among the Etruscans and the *Tyrrenoi* who, in the 6th century BC, still inhabited the Aegean and Anatolian coasts, was strong. It has recently been supported by studies of similarity of languages (e.g. the pre-Greek of the island of Lemnos), and by comparison of the DNA of Tuscan populations with that of some Anatolian groups.

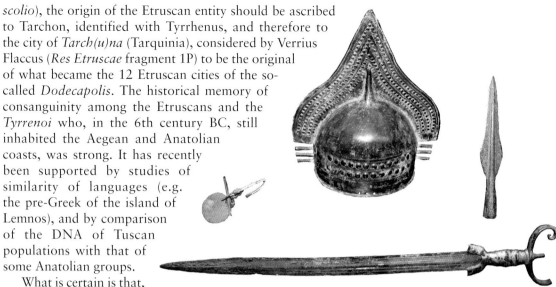

Equipment of an aristocratic warrior, late 9th century BC, from grave Monterozzi 3, Arcatelle necropolis, Tarquinia. These splendid finds are a Villanovan bronze crested helmet, a spearhead, an 'antennae' sword, and a *fibula* brooch. (National Archaeological Museum, Tarquinia; author's photo, courtesy of the Museum)

What is certain is that, after the Bronze Age, the Etruscan communities, independent but united in a confederation of 12 cities, dominated the political life of today's central Po Valley, Tuscany, Umbria and Lazio, and achieved supremacy over Rome in about the 6th century BC. Their maritime activity also brought them control of the main trade routes. In a battle of uncertain outcome, off the coast of Corsica in around 540 BC, an alliance of Etruscans and Carthaginians stopped the threat posed by the rival Phocean Greeks – founders of early 6th-century Massalia and Alalia – to the commercial expansion of coastal Etruria. In the early 5th century Etruscan maritime power and trade appear still to have been in the ascendant, but shortly afterwards the situation changed radically: Etruscan dominance at sea was broken in 474 BC by a heavy naval defeat off Cumae, inflicted on the fleet of the southern coastal cities by the triremes of Hieron of Syracuse.

The expulsion of the Etruscan kings from Rome, and the successive conflicts with the *Res Publica,* marked the beginning of the long twilight of the Rasenna. During the 4th and early 3rd century BC the Romans expanded slowly but relentlessly into Etruscan territory. In the second quarter of the 4th century Rome's principal enemy was the city of Tarquinia, while other cities of the Dodecapolis confronted the Romans from time to time in a subtle game of alliances and rivalries. In 359 BC the Tarquinii invaded Roman Etruria, soon being joined by the city of Falerii Veteres and – within two years – by the other central Italic Etruscan cities. After a fierce war the Romans prevailed, conquering both the Tarquinii and Falerii. Constant attrition with Gauls from the north and Latins from the south gradually wore the Etruscans down, and their military power and aspirations were eventually crushed by the Romans at the battles of the Vadimonian Lake (310 BC; Livy, IX, 39, 11) and Sentinum (295 BC). The Romans completed the final conquest of Etruria with the destruction of Volsinii in 264 BC.

However, when the Etruscans were absorbed by the Romans in the 2nd century BC the latter were already using symbols of power and political institutions inherited from their former enemies, and in the 1st century BC many noble Roman senatorial families proudly claimed ancient Etruscan origins.

CHRONOLOGY (BC)

900–750   Etruscan proto-history (Villanovan culture): formation of the early Etruscan peoples and their settlements, among which the powerful *Veii*, *Velch* (Vulci) and Tarquinii dominated their surrounding areas. The 8th century saw the development and economic growth in South Etruria of centres such as *Kaisra* (Caere, Cerveteri).

750–600   The 'Orientalizing Period': trade and wars with Greeks, Cypriots and Phoenicians. Formation of the archaic Etruscan culture and powerful urban aristocracy; flourishing of *Vatluna* (Vetulonia), and constitution of the Etruscan *Dodecapolis*.

730   According to Ephorus (Strabo, VI, 267), the Sicilian coasts are infested by 'Tyrrhenian pirates'.

670   Pitched battle near Fidene between the Romans led by Tullius Ostilius and a coalition of Etruscans, Fidenates and Albani.

600–480   The 'Archaic Period': expansion of Etruscan political domination.

616–509   Etruscan kings rule over Rome.

540   Naval battle of Alalia, between Etruscan/Carthaginian fleet and Phocean Greeks.

509 *et seq*   Expulsion of the Etruscan kings from Rome. Attempt by the Tarquinii family to restore their rule with the help of cities of Tarquinia and Veii; Porsenna, *lucumo* (king) of *Clevsi* (Clusium, Chiusi) temporarily restores Etruscan domination over Rome.

480   Beginning of the 'Etruscan twilight'.

474   Defeat of Etruscan fleet off Cumae, at the hands of Hieron of Syracuse.

450–400   The Samnites overrun Etruscan territory in Campania.

400–350   Gallic invasions of the Etruscan Po Valley.

395   The Roman consul Furius Camillus conquers Veii.

388–308   Revival of political and military power of Tarquinia under the family of Spurinnas, but the city is unsuccessful in attacks on Roman territories.

290   Defeat of the Etruscans by the Romans in the Third Samnite War.

280–264   Roman conquest of Etruria.

90   All Etruscan cities receive Roman citizenship.

THE VILLANOVAN ARMY

The warrior in Villanovan culture

In the 12th–11th centuries BC early groups of hunters made their appearance in the extensive territories between the valleys of the rivers Tiber and Arno, in the modern region of Tuscany and parts of Lazio and Umbria, where they occupied naturally defensible plateaux. It is likely that contemporaneous immigrations from Anatolia linked to the movements of the Sea Peoples impacted on this region. In the 9th century many communities took shape in Central Italy in a slow but continuous process which gave birth to the first cultural manifestation of Etruscan civilization; this is commonly termed 'Villanovan' after the discovery in 1853 of a large necropolis at Villanova/ *Velzna* near Bologna. Developing during the early Iron Age, this culture was extensively dispersed but shows homogeneous characteristics. During this period the weapons and thus the organization of warriors were transformed, some of them acquiring social importance and leadership functions.

Etruscan funerary rites included both cremations and interments, but the former were predominant in the early Villanovan period. After cremation, bones and ashes were placed in an urn covered by a bowl or helmet, the latter originally in terracotta but later an actual specimen in bronze. Along with the urn a number of other objects might be deposited in the tomb, such as spearheads, swords and cups. In this proto-Villanovan phase new kinds of weapons and ornamental objects made their appearance, e.g. the 'wing-axe', the long sword, and razors and *fibulae* brooches inspired by Oriental, Aegean and Central European models.

Military activity in the 8th century becomes even more evident from the deposition of entire bronze panoplies – helmets, shields, swords, axes, and horse bits. The apparent prosperity of Villanovan centres over time suggests that they did not practice an all-out warfare of conquest, but such grave finds confirm the fundamental importance, and thus the social elevation, of the warrior in these tribal societies. The beginnings of an oligarchic society (i.e. with military authority and economic resources concentrated in the hands of the few) are already visible in 8th-century funerary sites, especially in Southern Etruria. This process would give birth to a strong and restricted aristocracy – the so-called *principes Etruriae* of the Roman literary sources – whose power would be increased by external military conquests. The pattern

'Triangular' sword with tang ending in 'T'-shape, and bronze scabbard; first half of 8th century BC, from the Monterozzi necropolis, Tarquinia. (National Archaeological Museum, Tarquinia; author's photo, courtesy of the Museum)

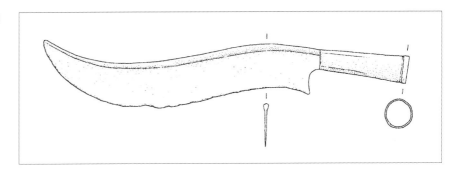

Knife dated to the 'Orientalizing Period', 8th–7th centuries BC, from Castiglione del Lago; British Museum. This category (type 8) shows a thin, serpentine blade with a thickened oval section along the back, and a separately made socketed handle of hammered bronze sheet. (Drawing by Andrea Salimbeti, ex Bietti-Sestieri and Macnamara)

of population in Etruria during the Villanovan and Orientalizing periods also lent itself to the mustering of armies: village communities with similar-sized populations were dispersed all across the territory in a consistent pattern.

Armies

War was the most complex activity undertaken by such small village communities, composed of a few family groups organized under their elders. The richest aristocratic class could afford a complete armament, and based its social supremacy on its warrior role, but diffusion of equipment in graves suggests that the lower class, too, increasingly bore arms due to an increase of external conflicts. In early-period graves shields are scarce; those of the late 8th century show growing numbers of shields, or of miniature copies symbolizing the status of men able to bear arms.

Not all adult males attained the rank of 'professional warrior': men were only rarely buried with swords rather than spears, suggesting marked social distinctions. From the Latin authors, and the Iguvine Tablets, it appears that military forces were divided into younger men with or without spears, and maturer men with or without swords.[1] We may reasonably guess that admission to an army brought not only risk but also social advantages: access to the politically active part of the community, the right to plunder, and a share of any land which might be conquered.

The aristocracy, the backbone of any army, were equipped with both defensive and offensive gear: bronze helmets, quadrangular bronze plates fixed by leather straps to the torso, large shields, lances, swords and daggers. The presence of lavish horse bits in some graves indicates that some of the

1 These seven bronze tablets, found at Gubbio, describe the religious ceremonies of the Umbrian Brotherhood, and hark back to practices of the early 1st millennium BC

 EARLY VILLANOVAN CULTURE, 9th–8th CENTURIES BC

(1) Leader with war-chariot, Tarchuna area
The early example of a war-chariot is from grave 15 at Castel di Decima, and the warrior is reconstructed partly from grave Monterozzi 3 in the Arcatelle necropolis, Tarquinia. This contained, among other objects, a crested helmet, an antennae sword, a spearhead and a *fibula*. His bilobate shield, of Aegean origin, is reconstructed after the fragmentary specimen from Brolio and the miniatures from grave XXI at Pratica di Mare; it lacks the typical ornamentation of the later Orientalizing Period. Chest-protecting bronze *kardiophylakes* are well attested. Note also the red 'war paint' used on the face and limbs by some Etruscans and Latins.

(2) Villanovan-Tarquinian axeman
The axeman is protected by the 'bell-helmet' from the Pozzo grave, Monterozzi necropolis; pairs of holes along the rim suggest the attachment of an organic-material lining, chinstrap and/or neck-guard. The oval shield is made of wood with leather covering, and has a raised wooden reinforcing rib with a central 'boss'. The use of necklaces and bracelets was widespread, but we do not know to what degree these were associated with military or civil fashions.

(3) Sardinian mercenary, Pupluna area
This mercenary, copied from the 'Teti archer' statuette, wears a low-profile horned leather helmet, a bronze breastplate and greaves. His main weapon is the long composite bow, made of wood, horn and sinew. Note the leather protector worn on the left forearm.

Late Early Iron Age Villanovan 'lunate' razors; British Museum. These show simple and more complex incised decoration; some finds have borne representations of figures. (A) Type 15, from Chiusi; 11.4cm (4.5in) long. (B) Type 16, from Bishop of Lichfield's sale. (C & D) Type 16, from Sir Henry Wellcome Collection; 12cm (4.7in) long; similar examples are attested in Bologna, Viterbo and Tarquinia. (Drawings by Andrea Salimbeti, ex Bietti-Sestieri and Macnamara)

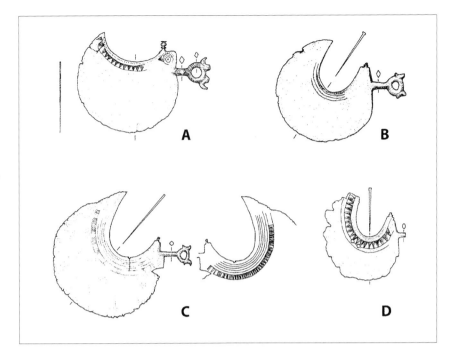

richer men fought on horseback. The lower class placed under the command of the elite warriors were modestly equipped, with wooden shields, spears, javelins, axes and daggers. The sword was probably the preferred weapon of the higher ranks; the fact that only some of the 'emerging' elders were armed with both sword and spear may therefore indicate that the ranks were arrayed according to an internal organization. Their deployment in battle may have been based on groups of modest numbers, formed by individuals

Bronze war axes, from Cortona: (left) 'winged' axe, so called from the shape at the shoulders, 10th century BC; (right) 'socketed-eye' decorated axe, 7th century BC. (Museo dell'Accademia Etrusca e della città di Cortona; author's photo, courtesy of the Museum)

of similar age under the leadership of the most experienced and valiant. This structure, divided in 'maniples' by age groups, reveals a first attempt at the organization of a 'psychologically spontaneous' group by the subdivision of growing village communities into *curiae*.

Tactics

Battles where the elders led the young into combat did not involve orderly linear formations or complicated tactics. If not simply ambushes, engagements would have been confused mêlées in which an exchange of javelins was followed by more or less brief hand-to-hand fighting, after which the winning side pursued and slaughtered their fleeing opponents before invading and sacking their village.

In the Villanovan army individual heroism was elevated above any concept of a compact battle array. After a first exchange of javelins and stones, warriors engaged the enemy using spears as thrusting weapons. After the first clash battles soon disintegrated into a series of single combats, in which the older fighters enjoyed the advantage of possessing short swords with triangular, ribbed blades. The whole panoply of the Villanovan warrior seems to suggest a mode of fighting in which physical strength and nimbleness were the most important factors; they were not enclosed in heavy, rigid armour, but were defended by the shield and a few protective elements localized on the body. Those who could afford to fight from horseback or chariots preferred the long sword with parallel edges called by archaeologists the '*antennae*' or 'Tarquinia' type. Cavalry was undoubtedly an effective strike force, capable of reversing the fortunes of an encounter and exercising control over long distances.

ARMS & EQUIPMENT

OFFENSIVE WEAPONS

Swords, daggers, axes, javelins and spears were of both bronze and iron. The massive introduction of iron for weapons production begun in Etruria in about 800–760 BC, probably under the influence of the Euboean Greeks. The bronze weapons were produced by fusion in moulds and then worked by

Axe-heads, Early Iron Age; British Museum.
BELOW LEFT
(A) First type, from Trasimeno; sub-type 42. (B) First type, from Maremma; sub-type 39. (C) Second type, from Bologna; sub-type 52.

BELOW CENTRE
(A) First type, from Tuscany; sub-type 38, 16cm (6.3in) long. (B) First type, from Populonia; sub-type 38, 20cm (7.9in) long. (C) Second type, from Grosseto; sub-type 61. (D) Second type, from Orvieto; sub-type 61.

BELOW RIGHT
(A, B, C & D) Second type, from Bologna; sub-type 62. (E) Second type, from Grosseto, Maremma; sub-type 52. (All drawings by Andrea Salimbeti, ex Bietti-Sestieri and Macnamara)

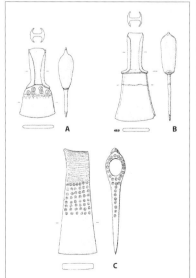
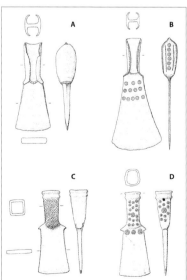
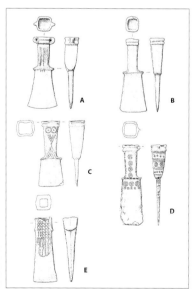

Iron spear and javelin heads, bronze razor and fragments, and *fibula*, from various graves at Volterra, 8th–3rd centuries BC. (Museum Guarnacci, Volterra; author's photo, courtesy of the Museum)

Early Iron Age spearheads of type 15, from Bomarzo near Viterbo; British Museum. These remarkable specimens are all of 97.4cm (38.3in) long, with thin 'flame'-shaped blades and conical sockets. Rows of decorative incised triangles are visible along the blade edges and (right) the midrib. A spearhead from Olympia in Greece is a very close parallel both in shape and size. (Drawing by Andrea Salimbeti, ex Bietti-Sestieri and Macnamara)

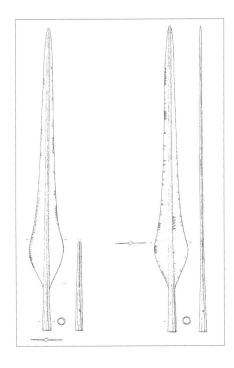

hammering, while iron ones were realized by hammering at high temperature metal bars produced in special ovens.

Swords and daggers

Villanovan-period swords show a continuity from specimens of the late Bronze Age. From these were derived all the types used by the Tyrrhenians during the Early Iron Age: the 'tongue grip' Italic and 'western grip' variants, and the 'antennae' swords. Scholars dispute the details of origin and diffusion, but it is clear that these weapons derived, in different variants in bronze and iron, from the prototypical so-called 'Naue II' swords of the late Bronze Age, where the smith introduced a strong hilt to improve earlier swords which had a narrow tang and no practical handle. The *Griffzungenschwerten* of the Early Iron Age were shorter than their prototypes (maximum 70cm/27.5 in).

The Italic 'tongue grip' swords had blades tending to a triangular shape, with various grooves parallel to the edges; their short length and sharp point suggests thrusting weapons. The prevalent typology in the Etruscan Villanovan area (specimens from Tarquinia) is the so-called Pontecagnano type, characterized by a triangular blade with lenticular section, a small rib and thin lines parallel to the edges, and lengths between 40 and 60cm (15.75 & 23.6 in). These date from the 9th to the 7th century BC, and differ from Bronze Age prototypes mainly in the semicircular shape of the upper part of the grip to which a two-part pommel was attached, and in having fewer rivet-holes (4–6) for attachment of hilt-grips of organic material. Attachment by metal wires and adhesives is also known, as in the sample from grave 495 at Pontecagnano. The 'western grip' type, characterized by a swelling/diminishing shape, has been attested only in a grave from Populonia/*Fufluna-Pupluna*, and this is clearly an import from Sardinia.

A third type, originating from Central Europe, was the 'antennae' sword with two parallel curling horns rising from the pommel. Beautiful 9th–8th century bronze specimens come from the Benacci Caprara necropolis (Bologna) and from Tarquinia. They have a parallel-sided blade tapering in to a point with a slight curvature; rarely, the blade is slightly curved for slashing. The scabbards were mainly in bronze, sometimes decorated with one or more discs. Some were of wood or leather covered with bronze sheet, decorated with embossed or incised geometric motifs or hunting scenes, and frequently with applied ivory or bone ornaments at the mouth. Expensive and elaborate scabbards, the straps often embellished with bronze pendants, are exemplified by an 8th-century specimen from Vulci (Osteria necropolis) whose mouth is decorated with a volute fitting ornamented with the images of two statuettes, or by the sword of the 'warrior of Prato Rosello'.

Bronze or iron daggers would have been much more common, varying in length between 25cm and 41cm (9.8–16in). Three main types are identified: (1) of bronze, with a short, wide triangular blade, and rivet-holes for fastening grips of organic material; (2) of iron, with a longer triangular blade, the handle part with an enlarged portion, fixed inside a hilt by rivets; and (3) of bronze, elongated triangular, cast in one piece with the hilt.

Normally less refined than swords, such weapons would have been simply attached to a leather or fabric waist belt, usually on the right side. However, one iron short sword from the first half of the 8th century BC was discovered near Volterra/*Velàthri* – tomb XIV, Guerruccia necropolis – together with decorated iron disks (diameter 8.6cm/3.4in) retaining traces of fabric inside, so probably elements of a suspension belt. The weapon's hilt was of bone reinforced with iron rings and copper decorations. Another beautiful Early Iron Age iron dagger with a bone hilt and bronze scabbard came from Veii. Daggers, swords and axes might also be worn thrust inside wide leather belts, sometimes plain but sometimes covered with embossed bronze plates; baldrics were also used, often decorated with bronze pendants.

A warrior's personal equipment also included general-purpose knives, and razors. Various knives discovered near Florence, Leprignano (in Latium) and Perugia and dating from the Orientalizing Period are 21.8–24.4cm long (8.4–9.6in); one has a slightly up-curving blade, and one from Vulci has the handle decorated with small 'swimming ducks' and concentric circles. Razors have been found with cast ring handles featuring two stylized birds' heads. Undecorated lunate razors with

(A) Early Iron Age leaf-shaped spearhead, probably deliberately bent over at time of deposition, and butt, from Castellani Collection. (B) Javelin head from Arezzo, British Museum; the faceted socket has two lateral pinholes, (Drawing by Andrea Salimbeti, ex Bietti-Sestieri and Macnamara)

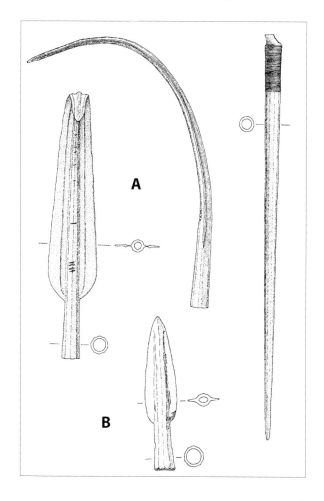

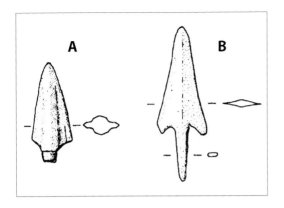

Late Early Iron Age arrowheads, (A) from Perugia and (B) from Orvieto; British Museum. (Drawings by Andrea Salimbeti, ex Bietti-Sestieri and Macnamara)

wide, almost circular 9.8cm (3.8in) blades have been found in Siena (*Seina*), Volterra and Viterbo (*Surina*).

Axes

Being cheap and easy to produce, axes were widely used weapons. While the shaft length must have varied, surviving blades measure 12–22cm (4.7–8.6in), of trapezoidal shape with straight or slightly tapering sides, and a slightly curved cutting edge. Many of these cast-bronze socketed axes came from Sardinia, in particular those with two pointed side projections (found also in the Balearic Islands, on the Italian and Iberian coasts, and even in Ireland). The axe, exclusively used by the infantry, decreased in utility with the increasing use of body defences, but the Etruscans developed models with longer shafts for two-handed employment. This obliged the user to carry his shield on his back, as shown on the warrior represented in the chandelier of the 'Circolo del Tritone' at Vetulonia/*Vatluna*. During the Orientalizing Period the use of a double-headed axe (*bipennis*) also begins to be documented.

Archaeologists classify Villanovan axes in two main types, depending upon the way the shaft was fixed to the blade (see drawings, page 11). 'First type' specimens have a divided socket open at both sides, which had to be hammered closed around a divided extension of the haft, while 'second type' axes have a single socket, giving a more secure fixing. Both types would have had bindings of metal wire or organic thongs.

Spears and javelins

Both thrusting spears and throwing javelins, for hunting and for war, are numerous from Italic sites, and they were clearly common among Villanovan armies. Study of remaining traces of the spear shaft in many sockets has identified acer, viburnum, hawthorn, pine, boxwood, beech and cornel wood, these latter also being used for axe shafts.

B **VILLANOVAN ARISTOCRATIC WARS, 8th–7th CENTURIES BC**

(1) Villanovan aristocratic cavalryman, Felzna area, 8th century

This cavalryman – partly reconstructed from grave 525, Askos Benacci, near Bologna – is protected by a crested helmet (from an example in Hamburg Museum), and has slung on his back a decorated bronze shield (example from Verucchio). His offensive weapons are a spear and the curved antennae 'sabre' from Bologna. Graves around Bologna have yielded a bronze prod for a horse, and a snaffle bit with chained and mobile elements with circular sections. The original terracotta horse showed a blue mane and tail, and red markings suggested tattoos or brands, perhaps with magical significance. These features are also found in other graves, e.g. the Tomba di Tori at Tarquinia.

(2) Proto-Etruscan leader, Narce area, 730 BC

Mainly obscured here by his cloak, the bronze armour of this senior leader, extensively decorated with repoussé work, is shaped like a 'poncho'; it is composed of one-piece front and back plates joined by straps under the arms. According to Cowan, it was shaped for an individual with very broad shoulders and a heavily muscled chest. His helmet, of crested type over a rounded bowl, is 43cm (16.9in) high, made of two sheets of bronze fastened partly along the crest by folding one sheet over the other.

(3) Villanovan leader, Tarchuna area, second half of 8th century

Reconstruction of the 'Corneto warrior' in his full panoply, to which we have added from another grave a *calotte* or cap-helmet, with decoration perhaps suggesting a human face. The Corneto skeleton possibly had an early example of linen corselet (*linothorax*), fastened with bronze buttons and hooks. It was reinforced with a bronze shoulder piece, and a rectangular breastplate decorated with gold foil and ornamented with stamped patterns of swimming ducks, stylized lotus flowers and other details. The shoulder guard worn on the right (the side not covered by the shield), recalls one from an Achaean grave at Dendra in Argolis; it retains traces of padding, confirming that parts of metal armour were lined with organic materials for comfort. The earlier Etruscan warrior custom of painting the face red would be retained by the Romans for some special ceremonies, in reference to the red-painted statue of Jupiter Capitolinus in the *statuarum praetextae* ritual.

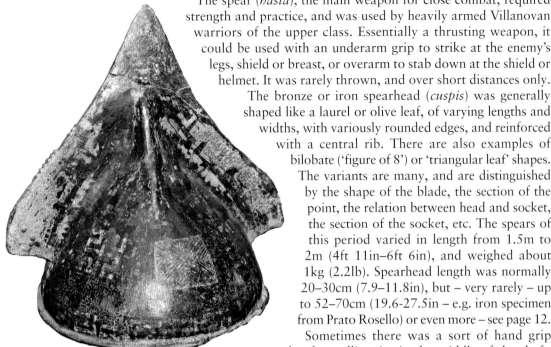

The spear (*hasta*), the main weapon for close combat, required strength and practice, and was used by heavily armed Villanovan warriors of the upper class. Essentially a thrusting weapon, it could be used with an underarm grip to strike at the enemy's legs, shield or breast, or overarm to stab down at the shield or helmet. It was rarely thrown, and over short distances only.

The bronze or iron spearhead (*cuspis*) was generally shaped like a laurel or olive leaf, of varying lengths and widths, with variously rounded edges, and reinforced with a central rib. There are also examples of bilobate ('figure of 8') or 'triangular leaf' shapes. The variants are many, and are distinguished by the shape of the blade, the section of the point, the relation between head and socket, the section of the socket, etc. The spears of this period varied in length from 1.5m to 2m (4ft 11in–6ft 6in), and weighed about 1kg (2.2lb). Spearhead length was normally 20–30cm (7.9–11.8in), but – very rarely – up to 52–70cm (19.6-27.5in – e.g. iron specimen from Prato Rosello) or even more – see page 12. Sometimes there was a sort of hand grip made of metallic wire in the middle of the shaft, or wire was used to secure the point to the shaft (e.g. an iron spear point, 37.2cm (12.6in) long, from Riparie necropolis, Volterra, first decades of 8th century). Most wire was bronze, but iron specimens are attested (Prato Rosello, Artimino/*Aritma*, 8th–6th centuries BC).

A metal butt or ferrule (*spiculum*), of Greek origin (*saurotèr*), was often employed to drive the weapon into the ground when not in use or to allow other movements of the arms, or might even be used as an emergency weapon. Ferrules were usually of bronze, polygonal or conical, and attached to the shaft by pins. One specimen 7.3cm (2.9in) long, classified as type 1, was found in Bolsena/*Volsinii*; this short, plain piece has a rounded tip. Another (type 3) from Orvieto, 10.2cm (4ins) long, has a distinct raised rim, faceted body with two pinholes, and a flat tip. One very long, slender specimen (sub-type 5) is of conical shape, 44.6cm (17.5in) long, with a distinct, slightly flaring rim, a lightly faceted body, pointed tip and no visible pinholes; an encircling band of incised lines decorates the upper part.

Among actual specimens of spearheads, not all have a plain, utilitarian appearance. One Early Iron Age example from near Florence has a conical socket and a narrow, foliate blade of rounded profile 29.9cm (11.7in) long. The faceted socket has a central facet extending beyond the junction with the blade, outer lateral angles at the base of the socket, and two lateral pinholes; there are also two small circular holes in the lower blade. The incised decoration is notable: on the blade, hatched triangles, wavy and zigzag patterns, circles and rows of dots encircling both holes and along the margins; and on the socket, opposed hatched triangles, circles, zigzag lines and rows of dots.

Some very large spearheads, measuring from 44.5–52cm (17.9–20.5in) long, now in the Castellani collection at the British Museum, came from Tarquinia and Bomarzo/*Polimartyum*. They have slender, conical, faceted sockets without pinholes, and long, narrow blades with slightly rounded

8th-century BC terracotta cover for a cinerary urn (i.e. for cremation ashes), shaped like a crested helmet decorated with bronze *lamellae* and metallic bosses. Such imitations were often decorated with the same type of geometric patterns as actual bronze specimens. This piece may be from grave 66 of the Monterozzi necropolis, location 'Fontanaccia', at Tarquinia. (National Archaeological Museum, Tarquinia; author's photo, courtesy of the Museum) lower parts and two wide lengthwise grooves; several oblique marks are visible on one side of the central ridge. When put in the grave some of them were bent, probably intentionally. Formally belonging to the Early Iron Age tradition of bronze weaponry, these specimens were found in important burials dating from slightly before and into the Orientalizing Period.

The javelin was mainly a throwing weapon, whose use required much practised skill on the part of a nimble warrior usually lightly protected with a small shield. It was used both on foot and horseback, and several weapons would have been carried. Men armed with two javelins are visible on a vessel from grave 23 at Stradello della Certosa (Bologna). The throwing distance was 40–50m/yards, less if thrown from horseback. Lengths were 85–90cm (33.5–35.5in), with a bronze point usually of conical or pyramidal shape, sometimes with lateral 'wings', whose length usually ranged from 18cm–30cm (7–12in), though an example from Arezzo measures 15cm (5.9in). Finds can therefore sometimes be confused with spear ferrules.

The sources also mention all-wood javelins, presumably with fire-hardened points. This cheap and essentially prehistoric weapon was used alongside bronze-headed spears from the 8th century; light horsemen also used short wooden darts about 60cm (24in) long.

Bows and arrows

Reasoning from the small number of bronze arrowheads that have been found, some scholars suggest that the use of the bow was very limited in the Villanovan world, or that it was employed more for hunting than in war. This may reflect the Homeric ideal of the aristocratic warrior, who scorned projectile weapons in favour of the glory of hand-to-hand combat.

The rare early arrowheads found are mainly of two types. One is shaped like an isosceles triangle with a straight or swallowtail base and a pointed or quadrangular tang; made of laminated bronze, it lacks a mid-rib. The other is of cast bronze, the olive-leaf blade having a mid-rib, with a strong quadrangular socket. Later and more advanced arrowheads have, whatever the shape, a conical or pyramidal socket. Some examples from Populonia show a small backwards projection on one side, which would act as a barb

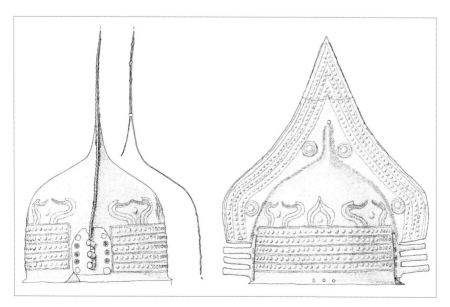

Bronze crested helmet of two-piece construction from Viterbo/*Vulci*, late Early Iron Age; British Museum. (Left) front/back view, (right) side view; it is 35.2cm (13.8in) high and 22.5cm (8.8in) in diameter at the rim. Note the embossed decoration, including, above the lower rows of bosses, what appears to be the outline of a crested helmet between two pairs of opposed birds' heads and necks. Three holes near the rim on both sides probably indicate the attachment of a chinstrap or lining; a fragment of coarse cloth was found inside the helmet from Monterozzi grave 1 at Tarquinia. (Drawings by Andrea Salimbeti, ex Bietti-Sestieri and Macnamara)

Round 'bell' helmet from Pozzo necropolis, Tarquinia; first half of 8th century BC; National Archaeological Museum, Tarquinia. This example is 21cm (8.3in) high and 23.5cm (9.2in) in diameter at the rim; note the 'spired' knob, drilled apparently for a plume. Made from thin sheet metal, Villanovan helmets needed thick padding or lining if they were to offer effective protection. The holes around the rims suggest its presence, and perhaps also a neck-guard and/or cheek-guards of organic material extending below the edges. (Drawing by Andrea Salimbeti, ex Hencken)

when the arrow struck flesh. In the so-called Chariot-Grave of Populonia (Orientalizing Period) very rare iron arrowheads have been found; these are 6cm long, with a diameter of 8mm (2.3 x 0.3in).

The simple bow of this period is represented on an 8th-century razor found in grave 16 at Benacci Caprara, Bologna. The presence of the composite recurved bow in the same period is attested on a razor from Vetulonia (Grosseto Museum), which shows a hunter drawing a bow in a shape resembling the Greek letter Σ (mentioned in the sources for the Scythian composite bow).

DEFENSIVE EQUIPMENT

Helmets, breastplates, shields and greaves were limited to the richer classes, and therefore constituted symbols of social and military authority. The excellence of Etruscan armourers is reflected in the tale of the creation of *ancile* shields by Mamurius for the Roman king Numa Pompilius, and attests to the expectations of their local patrons as early as the 8th–7th centuries.

Helmets

The helmet is well documented both in archaeology and iconography, and shows off the technical skills and aesthetic tastes of Villanovan craftsmen. The main types used during this period were the crested helmet (with pointed or round bowl – see Plates A1 and B2); the so-called 'bell' helmet rising to a spired knob (Plate A2); and a plainer so-called *calotte* type.

The bronze crested helmet takes its name from the characteristic quasi-triangular sheet which surmounts the bowl from front to back, following its contours most of the way down, below which triple sets of jutting bars were mounted front and back (this orientation is clearly shown on various statuettes (e.g from Este/*Atheste*). The exterior was generally decorated with embossing, inscribed geometric patterns or applications. This helmet,

C **'ORIENTALIZING PERIOD', NORTHERN ETRURIA, 7th CENTURY BC**

(1) Late Villanovan leader from Verucchio area
The presence of crested helmets in the Verucchio graves has led some scholars to suggest that this area was strongly colonized by Tarquinia or Veii, where such helmets were produced. The crest of this example is of painted horsehair mixed with gold threads, as attested by necropolis finds (e.g. grave Lippi 89). At this time the lords of Verucchio were armed with short iron swords in richly decorated scabbards, and ornamented axes. Leaning on his grounded spear is a shield with beautiful embossed decoration; his embossed armour is copied from the Basle Museum specimen.

(2) Rachu Kakanas, Vetulonian leader, with war-chariot
The grave of this named Rasenna-Etruscan *dux* of Vetulonia was one of the richest in military finds, including the remains of his two-horse chariot, reinforced with bronze disk *phalerae* of Orientalizing style. Leaning against the wheel, we show the interior of his circular bronze shield 84cm (33in) in diameter, probably manufactured in Tarquinia. His helmet has an extended hemispherical dome and a flared rim. His weapons included a richly ornamented dagger in an ivory scabbard, a spear, knives, and a trapezoidal axe. The plated belt is from examples such as those in drawings on page 27, and we have added a pair of greaves from a neighbouring grave. Note the sceptre, a symbol of command.

(3) *Lictor*, **Vetulonia**
The man in the lictor's grave was probably a soldier armed with a simple sword, axe and two knifes, but bearing on his shoulder the important symbol of the *fasces*, so was probably a royal guard. He wears a typical padded tunic of the period, and proudly brandishes his fasces, which has a total length of 60cm (23.6in). When different armies formed war alliances, it is believed that lictors were sent to the overall commander by other leaders as a sign of their temporary subordination.

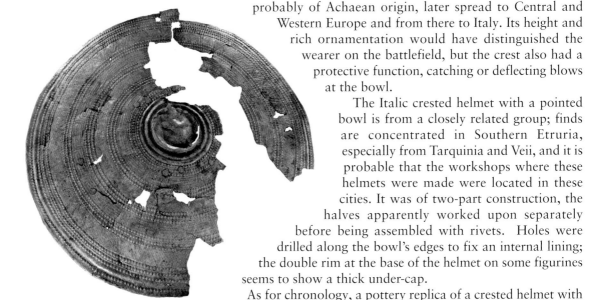

probably of Achaean origin, later spread to Central and Western Europe and from there to Italy. Its height and rich ornamentation would have distinguished the wearer on the battlefield, but the crest also had a protective function, catching or deflecting blows at the bowl.

The Italic crested helmet with a pointed bowl is from a closely related group; finds are concentrated in Southern Etruria, especially from Tarquinia and Veii, and it is probable that the workshops where these helmets were made were located in these cities. It was of two-part construction, the halves apparently worked upon separately before being assembled with rivets. Holes were drilled along the bowl's edges to fix an internal lining; the double rim at the base of the helmet on some figurines seems to show a thick under-cap.

As for chronology, a pottery replica of a crested helmet with pointed bowl found at Tarquinia in the Villanovan I A level might date back as far as the late 10th or early 9th century BC, while a bronze helmet of Villanovan IB (grave Monterozzi 3) dates from the 9th century. Another Tarquinian example may well be as early, and a third belongs to Villanova IC and dates from the first half of the 8th century (grave I, Poggio dell'Impiccato); two examples from Veii are also dated to that century. A few examples have been found more widely dispersed in Italy, and fragments of Italic crested helmets with similar decoration are known from Delphi and Olympia, probably either war booty taken by Greeks or votive offerings by Etruscan travellers.

The decoration of some helmets includes embossed representations of the foreparts of birds on the bowl, and bosses surrounded by concentric circles on the inner part of the crest. Beautiful examples of this kind of helmet come from Tarquinia (first half of 8th century), from Veii (tomb 871, necropolis of Canale del Fosso), and from Bisenzio/*Vesentum* (Le Buccacce, grave I – late 8th century), as well as the magnificent specimen from Poggio

Shield in bronze sheet decorated according to the Villanovan tradition, second half of 8th century BC, from Foligno, Colfiorito necropolis. (National Archaeological Museum of Umbria, Perugia; author's photo, courtesy of the Museum)

Reconstruction of a bronze shield from the so-called 'Corneto warrior's tomb' in Tarquinia, 730–720 BC. In several finds of bronze Villanovan shields (e.g. that from Verucchio) the remains of organic material survived, showing that they were constructed of several layers of leather covered by a bronze sheet. However, in this case a central handgrip is attached directly to the bronze, and pendant 'rattles' appear to have been fixed to the inside of the shield, perhaps for psychological effect. (National Archaeological Museum, Tarquinia; author's photo, courtesy of the Museum)

alle Croci (Volterra), dated to 725–700 BC. One of the most splendid examples, probably found in Vulci near Viterbo, is today in the British Museum, and shows the methods of construction and decoration (see illustration on page 17). The bowl and crest are made from two separate hammered sheets, joined at the base by two rectangular plates, which overlie and are riveted to both sides. The two sheets of the crest are joined at the apex and lower corners by three rivets with flattened heads, and by crimping along the outer edge. Both sides of the lower bowl are ornamented with five rows of large bosses, separated and bordered by double rows of small bosses; above these bands are embossed representations of a crested helmet between the confronting heads and necks of pairs of birds.

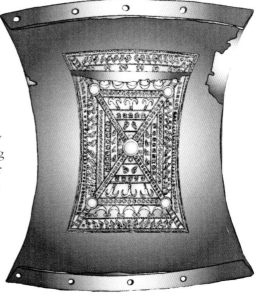

The crested helmets with round bowls come mainly from Veii, probably their main centre of manufacture. An example from Narce is made entirely of two sheets of bronze like the helmets with pointed bowls, though most crests of the others were made of separate sheets. How the crests were attached is hard to tell, but probably by soldering: no rivets are visible in the sufficiently preserved examples. In the Grotta Gramiccia specimen, grave 648, the crest was a single sheet of bronze; another example from Quattro Fontanili, grave AA10B (Veii), had a crest made of three parallel sheets of lead riveted together. The ornamentation on these helmets differs from that on those with pointed bowls, but often includes elements of the ridge-and-boss style. These helmets mainly belong to Villanovan IIB (the last quarter of the 8th century), even if a pottery representation of one from Tarquinia predates them by a century. This suggests that this type had earlier beginnings than the bronze finds indicate, and the two series of crested helmets in Italy may have overlapped in time.

The simpler *calotte* or cap helmet (see Plate B3) is well attested on the lids of cinerary urns. Hammered from a single sheet of bronze, it might show knobs or 'sockets' on the upper dome: decorative cast knobs (Veii, Grotta Gramiccia), and/or plain sockets which would have served for fixing feathers or horsehair crests. Specimens were found in Tarquinia, Populonia and Mantua/*Manth*. One of the most ancient comes from the Monterozzi necropolis (Tarquinia), dated between the late 10th and 8th centuries BC. Around the lower part are four rows of very small bosses with three rows of larger bosses between them. Above these a

Reconstruction drawing of a bronze pectoral plate from the same grave as the shield. It was found still on the breast of the buried warrior, who was covered by his shield. It shows holes along the curved upper and lower edges for attachment to a backing, and bears a highly decorated embossed gold sheet in the centre. Lines of birds – 'swimming ducks'? – are a popular motif. (National Archaeological Museum, Tarquinia; author's photo, courtesy of the Museum)

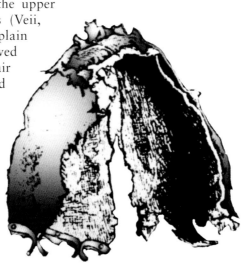

Reconstruction drawing of a bronze shoulder defence with linen lining, again from the 'Corneto Tarquinia warrior's tomb'. Its exact position on the body of the buried warrior is today unknown, but it measured 47cm (18.5in). Its only known parallel is a fragment 9.4cm (3.7in) long and constructed of joined iron lamellae, discovered in an 'Orientalizing Period' grave at Montagnola, Quinto Fiorentino. (National Archaeological Museum, Tarquinia; author's photo, courtesy of the Museum)

An armour disc, late Villanovan or early Etruscan, from Perugia; British Museum. The highly decorated hammered bronze sheet is 9.2cm (3.6in) in diameter, and has a strongly cast central attachment loop. It has been speculated that this may be a back-piece associated with the use of pectoral armour plates. (Drawing by Andrea Salimbeti, ex Bietti-Sestieri and Macnamara)

double arcade of tiny bosses has a medium-sized boss under each arch. Along the rim are pairs of holes that would have held the perishable material lining, a chin-strap, cheek-pieces, or neck-guard. The top socket, 6cm (2.6in) high, is decorated with horizontal lines; like those on Central European pieces it is cast on, but the knob at the top is flattened instead of spherical.

Another particular specimen, probably from Tarquinia (today in the Badische Landesmuseum, Karlsruhe) is a round 'bell' helmet with a 'spired' knob 19cm (7.5in) high, with a diameter at the rim of up to 23.5cm (9.5in). Each side of the rim shows three small holes, and both the front and the back another pair of holes. Above these are three rows of tiny bosses separated by two rows of larger bosses, and above the upper row of tiny bosses two more small holes are pierced both front and back. The knob is very clearly cast on. A curious bronze attachment, shaped like a trident bearing three little figures, was inserted in the top through a flange that exactly fitted a socket inside the top of the knob (the figures strongly resembling similar late Villanovan examples from Bisenzio). The bronze urn found together with the helmet helped to date it to the late 8th century BC. The most impressive examples of helmets without knobs or sockets are from Poggio dell'Impiccato (Tarquinia), where the helmet of Fossa Grave II shows magnificent frontal decoration giving the impression of a human face.

All these helmets left the face and ears exposed, limiting the protection but allowing good vision and hearing. Many originally had a plumed crest, sometimes attached directly (as on the simple calotte or 'pot' helmet), sometimes inserted in a metal crest holder. Horsehair, e.g. in the Vetulonia variant, was fixed between the two riveted halves of the crest.

Helmets of Villanovan type were used beyond the 8th century BC (Idice, Verucchio). Beside the bronze helmets that were probably distinctive of aristocrats, simple caps of thick leather might have been worn by common warriors. In some Villanovan centres, e.g. around Bologna, the total absence of metal helmet finds contrasts with images of fighting men apparently wearing such organic headgear. Models of these may be visible in the Caeritan urn-covers imitating war headgear; they show discs that have been interpreted as metal appliqués, which may survive as the bronze discs found in graves around Bologna, Bisenzio and Arezzo.

Shields
Metal shields are rare in all burials, and absent from the older graves. Their rarity can be explained by both their high cost and the widespread use of shields of wood and leather, such as ox hide. Precious bronze shields (like helmets) were kept by the families of the dead, and miniature representations were substituted for deposition in graves.

From the 10th century BC there are traces of the use of old bilobate shields of Aegean origin. Miniatures measuring up to 5.4cm (2.1in) were found in grave XXI at Pratica di Mare (Latium), comprising small concave bronze discs embossed with a double concentric row of dots, and retaining a decorated element to join two discs. These have some correspondence to a fragmentary find from Brolio – of uncertain date – which is preserved in Castiglione Fiorentino. This circular shield, made of a single sheet of bronze, is 54cm (21.2in) in diameter and slightly convex; it is decorated around the edges and in the middle with circles of small round bosses. The centre has no *umbo*, but is flattened and reinforced with large conical nail-heads. Though very thin, the edge does not show any evidence of reinforcement, and there is no sign of handles or grips.

Numerous representations of Villanovan shields allow us to distinguish two other basic typologies. The older model, characteristic of the 9th–8th centuries BC, was the so-called *scutum* of the Romans, attributed to the Sabines. Made of wood, hide or (rarely) of wickerwork, this is depicted as oval or elipsoid in shape, being carried beside more rounded or circular shields (Benacci Caprara necropolis, Bologna, grave 62). The 'Pozzo' grave at Poggio alla Guardia (Vetulonia) has preserved since the 8th–7th centuries a stone model of such an oval shield. It shows a single or triple rim, a central tripartite boss, and a surface divided in segments. Like late Celtic and early Roman specimens, this kind of shield had a vertical central reinforcement rib of wood, sometimes (but not always) furnished with a bronze boss, and might be covered with perishable material and decorated. The tapered reinforcing rib (*spina*) evolved into central shell-shaped, then *omega*-shaped bosses, as visible on the shields from the Regulini-Galassi tomb (Cerveteri) in the Gregorian Museum. Saulnier and Martinelli also agree on the existence of circular leather shields in Villanovan Etruria, probably made of *cuir bouilli*. A specimen from Verucchio (grave B, Orientalizing Period) was a simple wooden disc about 50cm (19.6in) in diameter, covered with bronze metal fittings representing warriors, lions and ducks. Round shields of these organic types appeared in Etruria before the 8th century.

Bronze horse bit, 8th century BC, from a warrior's grave at Poggio alle Croci, Volterra. (Museum Guarnacci, Volterra; author's photo, courtesy of the Museum)

The second type of shield to appear in the 8th century BC was round, slightly convex, and made of bronze. It probably derived from that of the Euboean Greeks, who adopted it from the Assyrians. Diameters varied from 50-60cm to 90-100cm (19.6–39.4in). It was fitted with a single double-T shaped metal handgrip riveted in the centre, and rings further out for shoulder belts. Beautiful examples of circular decorated bronze shields, with or without *umbones*, have been found in many Etruscan centres; about 60 specimens out of the 100 found in Italy come from Etruscan areas, mainly around Tarquinia, Cerveteri and Veii. At Casale Marittimo (tomb A, 8th–7th centuries) the shield is slightly convex, decorated along the edges with four lines of small round bosses, and in the middle with three lines of circles and three of small round bosses. The central area was without an *umbo* but was flattened, and reinforced with two small, round, flat plates.

Some of these shields evoked the decoration of those made of perishable materials. The bronze shield of Veii (grave 2079, found with a spearhead, a knife and other objects) had a central tripartite boss and a diameter of 72cm (28.3in), and was contoured by an iron wire designed to keep in place the organic layers forming the core of the shield. Rivets from an internal grip made of lead and bronze kept the *umbo* in place. The decoration formed small and larger triangles, exactly as on depictions of circular organic shields on a fictile helmet from Città della Pieve or Vetulonia. The bronze shield of the 'warrior of Corneto' bore vegetal decoration. (We should recall that wood, leather, wickerwork and bronze could be combined to produce a stronger shield.) Similar bronze shields decorated with several lines of small bosses, spirals, waves and circles were still employed in the Archaic Etruscan age; a 7th-century specimen is attested from the Petrina necropolis at Narce/ *Tevnalthia*.

Body armour and other defences

In Central Italy, especially in Etruria and Latium, the main protection of the warrior was provided by a metal pectoral plate (*kardiophylax*), though this was not so diffuse as the cuirass-discs of Central Southern areas. This plate was destined to protect the chest and heart, as suggested by its Greek name. It appears in the Villanovan area in around 760–720 BC, more or less contemporary with the introduction of bronze shields.

D **ETRUSCAN EXPANSION. 6th CENTURY BC**
(1) Lars Porsenna, *Lucumo* of Clevsin, with chariot
This is a reconstruction of the Etruscan king immortalized for generations of British schoolboys by Macaulay's poem *Horatius at the Bridge*. While there would have been some variations in their equipment, it is likely that the heavily-armoured *dynatotatoi* would have had a complete panoply: here, a full Corinthian helmet with high *lophos*, a painted 'bell-shaped' cuirass, protections for the thighs, and greaves decorated with embossed lion-masks. His cloak and helmet-crest are in purple and gold, symbolizing his royal power. The chariot is based on a splendid example from Monteleone da Spoleto, decorated with bronze panels representing the myth of Achilles.
(2) Rasenna hoplite of the first class, Clevsin
First-class hoplites wore defences similar to the Greeks, although produced by their own armourers. This high-status

warrior, copied from the Tomba della Scimmia (480 BC), has a Chalcidian helmet with Italic-style feather plumes flanking the crest. His early muscled cuirass shows red-lacquered shoulder-guards. He is otherwise protected by greaves, and by a *hoplon* shield decorated with a possible city blazon. His weapons are a spear and (obscured here) a curved, single-edged *kopis* sword.
(3) Etruscan horn-player
The simply-dressed hornist plays the precious specimen of a *cornu* now preserved in the Museo Nazionale Etrusco, Villa Giulia, Rome. This bronze horn is smaller than the later specimens of the Roman Imperial period; derived from prehistoric ox-horn instruments, it is almost circular in shape (*ex aere ricurvo*). The cross-brace in the middle, to help the hornist hold it steady, was not always present.

The simple metal pectoral would have covered the upper torso, in some cases also extending to the shoulders, and sometimes a back plate was also provided. De Marinis classified the many examples in two main types:

(a) An elliptic shape with equal opposite sides, concave or convex, usually undecorated (e.g. pectoral from Bolsena, grave 25). The maximum width is more than 27cm (10.6in), and the height slightly less. An exception with rich decoration is the bronze pectoral from the 'warrior's tomb' in Tarquinia (27 x 30cm/10.6 x 11.8in – see drawing on page 21).

(b) A simple quadrangular or rectangular form, sometime with rounded sides, always decorated with geometric motifs (e.g. pectoral from Tarquinia, Monterozzi necropolis, grave M9, 8th century BC). The sides are like (a) but less curved: straight and concave, straight and convex, two concave and two convex, or one straight and the others convex. The maximum width is less than 25cm (9.8in), the height similar or shorter (e.g. 16.8 x 14.5cm/6.6 x 5.7in pectoral in the 'warrior's tomb' from Prato Rosello, Artimino – the most northern Etruscan find). Others were found in Veii, Volterra and Verucchio. Interestingly, the Veii pectorals are formed of two identical sheets coupled with small flat-headed nails. Decoration was engraved or punched, as on the helmets.

Both types of plates had holes to fix the pectorals and back plates to a leather harness or corselet, being either hooked to vertical and transverse straps or sewn directly to a leather backing. The dimensions of the plates were intended to allow as much neck and waist movement as possible. The natural co-location of such plates would put the concave sides towards the arms.

A small piece of equipment in the British Museum collections may represent a very rare specimen of a round back plate of such a defence; urns of the classical Etruscan period show straps fastening such small disks on the centre of the back. Another round element, a pectoral, was found in

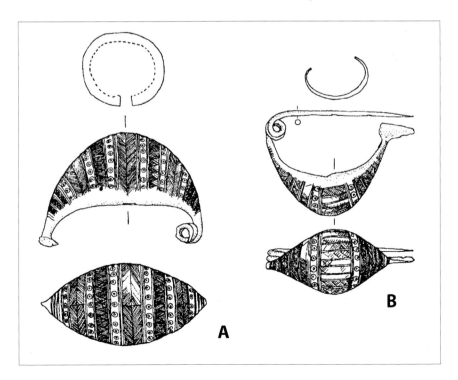

Early Iron Age *fibulae* of the 'rigid arch' type; British Museum. (A) from Perugia, 8cm (3.1in) long; (B) from Orvieto, 7.3cm (2.8in) long. (Drawings by Andrea Salimbeti, ex Bietti-Sestieri and Macnamara)

Verucchio (grave 89). Like some conventional pectoral plates, these cuirass discs presented a series of movable rivets intended (like a specimen from Bolsena, grave 25, La Capriola) to fasten a ring reinforcement on the back. In this specimen, reconstruction of the width of the cross-strap (14cm/5.5in) was possible thanks to a small supporting string. In such cases the cross-strap supporting the pectoral was probably protected by rivet-heads.

One very rare surviving Etrurian breastplate preserved in Basle (see Plate C2) is from a complete bronze cuirass dated to the 8th–7th centuries BC and showing affinity to the embossed bronze European armours from Fillinges. Another unusual form is represented by the bronze 'poncho' cuirass from Narce (University of Philadelphia Museum), and, in gold and copper, from the Regolini-Galassi tomb from Caere. Possibly of Aegean origin, these anticipate the complete suites of armour used by the later Etruscans, but are linked to particular groups; they may be identifiable with the bronze breastplate (*aeneum pectoris tegumentum*) used by the Salii priests of Archaic Rome. A possible linen version of this type, perhaps reinforced with metal strips, can be seen on the famous 'warrior vase' from Mycenae.

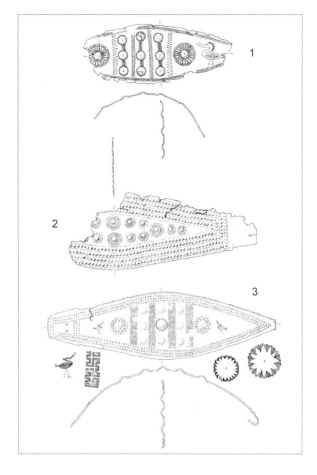

Late Early Iron Age elliptical bronze belt-plates; British Museum. (1) Note the incised crested bird. (2) This fragment, 33cm (13in) long, shows at the right a surviving hole for attachment to the belt's fabric. The embossed decoration recalls that of sheet bronze objects of the Villanovan II Period. (3) This plaque measures 40cm by 11cm maximum width (15.7 x 4.3in); note attachment holes at left. The decoration is varied, featuring bosses, sun discs, birds, and squared bands of 'trident' patterning. (Drawings by Andrea Salimbeti, ex Bietti-Sestieri and Macnamara)

Villanovan warriors also wore defences of padded leather, and sometimes the only protections worn were wide, elliptical bronze plates on waist belts (*cincturae* – see Plate C1). Most of the Italic specimens come from central and southern Etruria (Corneto), but examples are also known from the Po Valley. Although such protection was known during the Villanovan I period, most examples with contexts come from tombs of the Villanovan II. Usually the elliptical hammered belt plaque had a deeply curved shape, with a hooked terminal at one end and holes for attachment to the fabric of the belt at the other. Towards each end of the plate a crested bird might be incised, and (rarely) rows of bosses might follow the edges. Such bronze facings for belts of leather or other materials covered the front part of the waist, like the decorated ones represented on two statues of prince-warriors from Casale Marittimo (7th century BC).

Greaves are attested from some pairs of oval shape having a horizontal convex section, like the examples from Veii dating to the second Villanovan phase. These greaves followed pre-Villanovan models found in Central Europe, the Carpathians and the Aegean region.

Cavalry and chariots

Villanovan finds confirm fighting horsemen and war-chariots, reserved for the leaders. The horses were sometimes sacrificed on the death of their master, following him into the tomb in accordance with a custom also practiced on Cyprus. Their harness included finely decorated bits made of bronze; several were found at Veii, which may well have been a centre of their manufacture, but they principally come from Southern Etruria with rare examples from further north. The former come from graves of the Veii II phase, though later examples are known. Beautiful bronze bits with horse-shaped lateral elements have been attested in Accesa near Massa Marittima (8th century BC).

Chariots were articles of great luxury and high prestige. A bronze cruciform element interpreted as a possible separator for chariot reins has been dated to the first half of the 8th century (tomb XIV, Guerruccia necropolis near Volterra), though the oldest attestations of chariots intended principally for military use are models from Tarquinia (Selciatello di Sopra, grave 44) of the mid-9th century BC. The greatest diffusion of two-wheeled chariots occurs between the Villanovan and Orientalizing periods, and all the way up to Archaic times. Important specimens have been found in Vulci (necropolis of Osteria) and Vetulonia (Circolo del Tridente, 8th–7th century). In the graves, the usual armament associated with the chariot is two or three spears.

Symbols of rank

The decorated metal 'poncho' cuirass from Narce (see Plate B2) is an exceptional find for this era; certainly reserved for a wealthy and powerful leader, it symbolized his status as well as providing physical protection. Rich warriors also exhibited another luxury item of military equipment: the metal 'canteen' worn on a strap across the shoulder, presumably during long marches or campaigns (see Plate B3). These splendidly decorated bronze flasks have been found in various localities including Tarquinia and Vetulonia. Again, their degree of ornamentation goes beyond any practical use, and may be considered symbolic of the owners' rank; men of lower classes normally used flasks made of animal skin.

Other lavishly decorated objects worn by high-ranking warriors included necklaces, pendants, brooches, bracelets and rings, mainly of bronze or valuable metal, or decorated with amber, glass or bone. (Some may even have been awarded for bravery, as the Romans later did.) Some bracelets, like examples from Vetulonia, demonstrate a filigree technique invented by the Etruscans.

Finally, the axe was already employed as a symbol of power and for ceremonial purposes. A strange ceremonial specimen was found near Volterra (grave H1, Casale Marittimo necropolis, early 7th century). This object was

ETRUSCAN WARS WITH ROME, 5th CENTURY BC

(1) Roman *tribunus* Aulus Cossus, 437 BC
This officer is based on accounts by Livy and on the bone plaques from Praeneste showing Latin hoplites. He is armed with a spear and a two-edged *xiphos* sword, and carries a round *clipeum* shield. The crest and diadem of his Attic-type helmet are (hypothetically) shown here in the same colour. His leather muscled armour is copied from the Roman warrior depicted in the so-called 'François Tomb'; it was probably moulded and hardened by the *cuir-bouilli* technique that would be used until the Middle Ages.

(2) Tolumnius, *Lucumo* of Veii
Livy (IV, 17-19) and Plutarch (*Romulus*, XVI) give us important attestations to the employment of the *linothorax* by an Etruscan

king. Following the single combat between King Tolumnius of Veii and Aulus Cornelius Cossus in 437 BC, the former's linen armour was dedicated at the temple of Jupiter Feretrius: '...Then he [Aulus] despoiled the lifeless body, and cutting off the head stuck it on his spear, and, carrying it in triumph, routed the enemy... He solemnly dedicated the spoils to Jupiter Feretrius, and hung them in his temple... Augustus Caesar ...read that inscription on the linen cuirass with his own eyes.'

(3) Rasenna archer
The use of the composite recurved bow (*arcus sinuosus*) is attested on painted plaques of the Tarquinii period; constructed of bonded wood and horn, it would have required great strength to draw. Vergil quotes the Etruscan archers using the quiver or *leves gorytus* (X, 168).

made of three bronze axe heads measuring 20cm (7.9in) cast together, and attached to an S-shaped maplewood shaft 90cm (35.4in) long, wrapped along its whole length with a bronze strip decorated with several small ducks. This ceremonial tool was placed on the chest of the dead, and the absence of other weapons in the grave supports the hypothesis of its being a symbol of power. It was probably the ancestor of the *fasces*; the three axes had a hole under the junction-point through which passed a bronze fastening-ring. In the chariot-burial of grave A at Casale Marittimo the chariot was accompanied by a helmet, dagger, sword, two iron spears, and also a group of highly decorated bronze and iron axes united together like those in grave H1 at Casale Marittimo. The archaeological documentation suggests that in the Orientalizing Period bronze axes identified elevated military rank.

Clothing

Villanovan warriors wore simple tunics decorated only with coloured lines and dots. Coarse fabrics often showed geometric patterns, which were the dominant ornamental motif of the time. Among the military clothing of the Early Etruscans the ancient sources mention the *tebenna* (*tèbennos*, Dion. Hal. III, 61), a heavy coloured cloak that was possibly an ancestor of the Roman *toga* (Servius, *Ad Aen*. II, 781). Another rounded cloak known as the *laena* could be worn by warriors; Sekunda suggests that this was derived from the Greek *chlaina*.

The typically Mediterranean habit of total or partial male nudity was known in the Villanovan and Etruscan world, although surely not as an everyday practice. Men frequently went bare-chested, with loincloths and handsome pointed boots. Whatever the precise form of dress, it would have been secured with bronze *fibulae*, which have been recovered in quantity from warrior graves. Particularly famous are those found in the necropolis of Vetulonia, which demonstrate the technique of granulation. Etruscan *fibulae* can be divided into two main classes: (a) a rigid arch, fixed to the tongue with a simple spring, which lasted until the Roman period; and (b) the so-called 'snake' shape, lacking a rigid arch – this is the more ancient type, and already appears in shaft-tombs. Beautiful samples of rigid-arch brooches are attested in Orvieto and Perugia. One specimen of an intermediate type is a silver 'pins-and-buttons' *fibula* found in the 'warrior's tomb' at Corneto, which includes five filigree sections. Other examples in bronze or electrum have the 'snake' body enlarged, or with pointed or 'stick-and-globe' protuberances.

The later Roman practice of indicating rank by distinctive shapes and decorative elements in footwear can also be traced back to the Etruscans. Statuettes show soft leather calf-length boots with raised, pointed tips and closed with frontal laces.

THE ETRUSCAN CLASSICAL ARMY

Social and political evolution

The Villanovan communities of Southern Etruria, which lived in large agglomerations on new routes of trade and communication, were slowly transformed into major cities (e.g. Tarquinia, Veii, Vulci and Vetulonia), and experienced a spectacular flowering during the 7th century BC. The presence of rich mining deposits furnished silver, copper and iron, and trading contacts throughout Italy and the wider Mediterranean brought to the Villanovan people luxury items and wealth. This encouraged ambitions for conquest, and a consequent growth of military culture. (In Northern Etruria, on the other hand, the aggregation of communities seems to have been slower and less striking.)

The Early Iron Age communities of Southern Etruria soon controlled thousands of square kilometres, and began to elaborate the concept of citizenship. At the end of the Villanovan period, after external conquests, internal conflicts increased the concentration of riches and political power, of which the military element was a fundamental support. Commercial and economic expansion led to a strongly oligarchic society, in which a rich and powerful urban aristocracy (the *principes*) imposed themselves over the lower classes. The concentration of religious, political and military power is visible in the recorded names of magistrates and priests.

Etruscan helmet of Negau typology, early 5th century BC, from Arezzo. (Museo Archeologico Gaio Clinio Mecenate; author's photo, courtesy of the Museum)

When the Etruscans started to become sailors and merchants they were obviously more exposed to external attack, and threats from the Celts and Romans obliged the Rasenna to create more efficient military structures. Their organization is not yet completely clear, but considering the strong Hellenic influence we can suppose that their early military institutions corresponded basically to the Greek model. The *libri rituales* of each community described their military institutions, but survive today only in fragments from the works of classical authors.

Starting from the 7th century BC, each urban nucleus gained enough independence to create a distinct army. In this period the Etruscans, particularly those of coastal and Southern Etruria, adopted the Greek method of fighting. Diodorus (XXIII, 2) states that in the first engagements between the Romans and Tyrrheni the latter fought in phalanx formation. Again, according to Athenaeus (VI, p. 231), the rank formation (στάδια μάχη) was adopted from the Tyrrheni, who attacked in a phalanx. (Both these authors probably relied on the text of the *Ineditum Vaticanum*.) However, the Etruscan phalanx was not a slavish copy of the Greek model.

The best equipped warrior was the aristocratic hoplite, about whom we have a good deal of evidence from material culture, such as an *oinochoe* from Ischia di Castro (Villa Giulia Museum). The lower classes provided more lightly equipped warriors. In peacetime the hoplites assured the defence of cities and ports, and served as marines. In the cities they were flanked by a sort of 'city guard' that policed the city gates, traffic and shipping. Greek mercenaries may have promoted this social evolution, including those serving in the navy and those building fortifications. The northern and inland cities, more subject to Italic and Celtic influence, were slower and more limited in making these changes.

Because the Etruscan cities were socially less compact than the Greek ones they had more difficulty in maintaining a large number of professional

Front view of a highly decorated Negau helmet from Lombardy, 5th century BC; this magnificent completely-cast helmet is a northern version of that in the Lanuvium panoply. The divided crest-holder on the apex is shaped like a duck. The upper part of the bowl is decorated with a floral motif; the lower, with the head of a divinity above big, sweeping eyebrows and eyes with inserted blue glass pupils; and the rim, with a repeating pattern of spiral shells. (Antikenmuseum, Berlin, inv. 30 018a; photo courtesy Andrey Negin)

Etruscan-made bronze Negau and Corinthian helmets, 474 BC, from Olympia, Greece. Helmets found in the sanctuary at Olympia bear Greek inscriptions: *'[From] Hiaron the Dinomenides and the Syracusans to Zeus [booty] from the Tyrrhenians from Cuma'* – i.e., these are war trophies from the naval battle of Cumae in that year. (Archaeological Museum, Olympia; author's photos, courtesy of the Museum)

warriors, and envisaged the recruitment of certain classes only in emergencies. As a consequence the hoplites, or heavy infantry always in arms, were a minority elite. However, during the 6th century a profound change took place, when the lower classes began to exert pressure to be admitted to the army and, accordingly, to active political engagement. It was perhaps in this period that the army was divided into classes corresponding with wealth in land, as described by Livy (I, 43) for the Etruscan Roman army of Servius Tullius:

(a) A first class of heavy hoplites, with bronze helmet (*galea*), round shield (*clipeum*), greaves (*ocreae*) and cuirass (*lorica*), sword and spear.

(b) A second class similarly armed, but with only a bronze pectoral as protection, and carrying an oval *scutum* instead of the hoplite *clipeum*.

(c) A third class similarly armed, but without pectoral. In the battle array the second and third classes flanked the first one, whose main duty was to keep the gaps in the front ranks filled and to pick the right moment to break the enemy ranks.

(d) A fourth class of light warriors armed only with javelins; mainly mercenaries, these were entrusted with scouting, skirmishing, and flank protection. The employment of mercenaries (μισθοφοροι) is attested e.g. in the passage of Dionysius (V, 14-15) describing the preparations by the Tarquinii for war against Rome. Some cities willingly sent citizen troops, but others sent mercenaries or any other available men in order to fulfil their obligations towards the Tarquinii.

(e) A fifth class armed with slings and stones, which also included the *cornicines* and *tubicines* (musicians).

However, this particular model of organization cannot be applied generally to the 12 cities of the Dodecapolis. Normally the king or *rex* (*lucumo*, Latin word from the Etruscan *lauchume*) was the leader of a community which was divided into *curiae* (family groups or *gentes*) mainly for the purposes of the military levy. In Etruria, as in Rome, kings exercised the *imperium domi militiaeque*, i.e. both civil and military power. All the cities had their *lucumones*, and when the confederation went to war one king among them was elected as commander of the whole army, each city sending a *lictor* to him as a sign of their obedience. The armies were commanded by important representatives of the city oligarchy. These generals and admirals were in charge of the defence of cities and ports, war fleets, army organization, logistics and armament. In the Etruscan language they were called *zilath*, with the addition of *maghister* or *purth*. There was a difference between the two: probably the *purth* was the field general, while the *zilath* was the supreme magistrate of the state, corresponding to the Latin *praetor*. We do not know how many generals or military officers were present in a single city's army, but this was probably determined by the size of each city-state. In any case, on the battlefield responsibility was normally held by a single man with his subordinate officers (though joint operations with other cities may have complicated the chain of command).

Fresco showing Achilles ambushing Troilos, 530–520 BC, Tomba dei Tori, Tarquinia. The hero wears a Corinthian helmet. Although the painting is now indistinct, under close examination it offers an interesting example in Etruscan art of a warrior brandishing a curved *kopis* sword. (Author's photo, with permission of the Soprintendenza dell'Etruria Meridionale)

Etruscan Pilos-type bronze helmet, mid-4th century BC. As well as the two surviving lateral tubes for side-plumes there was once a third crest-support, now missing. Etruscan warriors wearing Pilos helmets are visible on the 4th-century 'Amazons Sarcophagus' from Tarquinia. (Etruscan Gregorian Museum, Vatican City; author's photo, courtesy of the Museum)

Detail of depiction of Etruscan hoplite with Attic helmet, linen armour and shield, from the 4th-century 'Amazons Sarcophagus'. The uncropped image also shows bronze greaves with muscle embossing. (Archaeological Museum, Florence: author's photo, courtesy of the Museum)

The Etruscans never succeeded in putting large armies into the field; class tensions dictated that not all classes bore arms, and most of a city's inhabitants were not warriors but tradesmen and craftsmen. Furthermore, many of the cities were mainly autonomous or even rivals, and there was no means of anticipating the number or quality of troops who would turn out for any particular battle. The structure of the Etruscan confederation of cities lent itself to the creation of local militias rather than large armies under unified command, which required a more efficient and consistent organization. Some scholars also attribute Etruscan military shortcomings simply to relatively small populations.

According to Propertius (IV, 1, 29) the Etruscan kings were the first to adopt a regular military camp for the army. Furthermore, 'a well organized siege camp made with wooden structures was given as a gift by Porsenna to the Romans after having agreed the peace with them' (Dion. Hal. V, 34).

Organization

In the late Etruscan period the very distinct stratification of society influenced the military structures. Almost until the end of the Etruscans' identity as a people the aristocracy claimed their right to lead the armies, basing their claim on martial skill and leadership. They alone had the authority and resources to summon and (presumably) to arm troops, and take to the field. A rather old-fashioned method for levying armies would have been reflected on the battlefield in a number of ways.

In his description of the army of the Veii confronting the Romans in 480 BC, Dionysius (IX,5, 4) writes that the Roman consuls were taken aback by its size (πλήθος) and by the quality of its weapons (τήν λαμπρότητα τῶν ὅπλων). The army of Veii itself was augmented by the chief men of rank *(hoi dynatotatoi)* from other cities throughout Etruria, who had brought their own clients and dependents *(penestes)*. The word *penestes* probably refers to 'vassals', above servile status but obliged to supply agricultural labour and military service to a specific *dynatotatos*, clan or family. In his turn the dynatotatos was under some sort of a personal or family obligation to whomever was raising an army to fight for the city. The summoning of confederate armies presumably relied upon family connections between the dynatotatoi of different cities (Livy, II, 6). The fact that clans within a city could send troops to fight on behalf of the clan and not the city must have diminished the authority of city institutions while elevating that of the individual aristocrat and his clan.

It is probable that the dynatotatos himself was responsible for equipping his men, and that his status was reflected by the number of troops he could supply and their military equipment. It is unlikely that the various elements of an army were trained together or uniformly armed; rather, it was composed of two distinct groups, the aristocracy and the vassals, each with narrowly defined functions. The penestes were fully armed, and would have been equipped with a round Etruscan helmet, a sword or axe, and perhaps a shield. Nevertheless, it is likely that some would have had only a helmet and one offensive weapon. Livy (IX, 37,12) mentions farmers recruited by their masters and armed to fight the Roman looters who attacked Etruscan territory from the Cimini Mountains at the end of the 4th century BC. In such circumstances light armament would have necessitated fighting in loose formations, and combats between individuals.

3rd-century BC Etruscan Phrygian helmet from Castiglione del Lago, Sigliano, showing rich floral and vegetal embossed decoration. (National Archaeological Museum of Umbria, Perugia; author's photo, courtesy of the Museum)

Tactics

The strong Greek and Oriental influences on the art and material culture of Etruria from the second half of the 7th century BC onwards extended to the organization and tactics of armies. The contemporary organization of society into *gentes* formed the basis for a perfunctory ordering of and hierarchy within units, although the size of individual forces initially remained small and their battle tactics simple, with considerable differences in the weaponry carried being dictated by individual preference and finances.

The basic tactic, upon the Greek model, was the phalanx – a continuous line of hoplites armed with long spears, with its wings protected by cavalry. Connolly believes that we can say with confidence that Etruscans adopted the old *lochos*, with its 8 ranks and 12 files of hoplites. In the Museo Barracco a 5th-century stele from the Chiusi region shows such warriors advancing to battle, followed by their attendants; they wear crested helmets with earpieces, armours and greaves – the classic equipment of the heavy infantryman. Among the support units it is worth mentioning the socially humble slingers, who took part in operations from the margins of the battlefield. Their presence alongside the more or less heavily armoured infantry and cavalry made Etruscan armies complex and diverse forces with considerable fighting power.

Detail from black-figure decoration by the 'painter of Micali', c.510 BC, on a pottery *olpe* from Tarquinia. The scene suggests a departure for war or a training session. In all it shows seven hoplites marching forward in rank formation, protected by high-crested Chalcidian helmets and Argive shields decorated with typically Etrurian embossing. At left is a young musician blowing a *cornu*; his role might perhaps be likened to that of a drummer-boy in later European armies. (National Archaeological Museum, Tarquinia; author's photo, courtesy of the Museum)

The aristocratic warriors who rode out on horseback would have served as the scouts, and in battle would have engaged other cavalry; it seems probable that the Etruscans employed their cavalry as a distinct branch of the army. Some slabs of 6th-century terracotta friezes manufactured in Southern Etruria in Archaic style – found in both Etruria and Latium – represent warriors on horseback accompanied by 'squires' similarly mounted. (The shields are those of infantry hoplites, prompting some scholars to suggest that these are not cavalrymen but 'mounted infantry'.) We know that the *equites priores* of Tarquinius Priscus took the field with two horses, one ridden by the *eques*, the other by the squire. Granius Licinianus writes (XXVI, 2) 'I shall not fail to mention the horsemen, which Tarquinius doubled so that the *priores equites* led into battle two horses apiece'. The expression *equites priores* allows one to postulate, as Helbig points out, the parallel existence of *equites posteriores*, i.e., horsemen with only a single mount, which was used in an emergency by the *eques prior*, or his *armiger*, or both.

THE LAST WARS, 4th CENTURY BC

(1) Aristocratic Rasenna woman
This Etruscan lady is copied from the Tomba dell'Orco frescoes, and is dressed in the common fashion of 'Magna Graecia': a garlanded headdress, discoid earrings, a long cloak over a pleated linen tunic, and *calcei repandi* on her feet.

(2) Rasenna hoplite from Velzna
Reconstruction of the warrior from the Settecamini tomb near Orvieto, which yielded a Montefortino-style helmet, a shield and a muscled cuirass. Archaeological fragments of Etruscan shields from graves in Perugia and Settecamini give us clear evidence for the heavy phalanx style of fighting in the 5th–4th centuries. The central position of the *porpax* arm-loop shows that it passed around the arm just below the elbow (see G1), with a handgrip near the rim; this was useful only in the linear 'shield wall' formation typical of the hoplite phalanx.

(3) Rasenna hoplite from Tutere
One of the most spectacular statues of warriors, the nearly life-size 'Mars of Todi' dated to about 350 BC, shows the employment of lamellar armour. The lamellae could be in bronze or – as suggested by their white colour in many artistic representations – of white metal, or even of an organic material such as bone.

The sources are poor in descriptions of Etruscan battles involving very large arrays, and anyway these were not required by the wars of that period. An aristocratic way of fighting seems to be attested for the 7th century, and some iconography presents heavily armed men engaged in single combat, archers, cavalry, and warriors riding out in chariots in the Homeric tradition. A tendency of the dynatotatoi to engage in *monomachia* (single combat) with others of similar rank is supported by depictions on sarcophagi and wall paintings. The warriors' wealth is evinced by elements like horses or armour, and their skill by the training needed to handle horses, chariots, bows or close-quarter spears. An example of such an episode is the mounted duel at the battle of Silvia Arsia between the Roman *praetor* Brutus and Aruns, the son of Tarquinius the Proud.

Although not fielding large armies the Etruscans often achieved important successes by moving fast and attacking an enemy near his main centres, as happened at Syracuse. It was only in the final period of Etruscan history that the threat posed by Rome obliged them to recruit large armies, and – because in their last wars against Rome the Etruscans acted in alliance with the Gauls and Samnites – it is difficult to know in detail what tactics they then employed.

Maritime power

The Etruscans recognized that control of the Tyrrhenian Sea was fundamental to the protection of their north-south trade routes. They employed ships equipped with single or double banks of oars; the sources tell us that Etruscan seamen were much feared, and renowned for legendary exploits (such as the theft of Hera's statue from the island of Samos). The Greeks considered them pirates for their bold deeds in the Mediterranean. The so-called 'vase of Aristonothos', probably made in Caere by a Greek artist in around 650 BC, is considered by several scholars to depict sea warfare between Etruscans and Greeks. It shows a clash between a large *pentecontor*-type ship against another warship equipped with a ram. Both vessels visibly carry warriors with spears, crested helmets, and large decorated shields. Another depiction from an Etruscan vase dated 500 BC is a black picture made by the 'Micali painter', showing a ramming vessel on which running warriors and archers seem ready to board an enemy ship.

A rough mid-4th century Etrusco-Chalcidian helmet of the Vulci variant type; note ring at apex, and disc on rim. (Etruscan Gregorian Museum, Vatican City; author's photo, courtesy of the Museum)

ARMS & EQUIPMENT

Although the organization of later Etruscan armies is still a matter of work in progress, we have good evidence for their offensive and defensive equipment thanks to numerous archaeological finds. These, particularly those from Southern Etruria and Latium, confirm a high level of quality relative to those of many contemporary Italic peoples. Bronze, iron and other metals were in

Details from an amphora from Pescia Romana, of the Tyrrhenian Group dated to 575–550 BC, showing the killing of Troilos by Achilles (left). He alone is depicted wearing a bronze so-called 'bell' cuirass, and carrying a *dyphilon* shield of Boeotian typology. The other figures carry Etruscan *episemata* shields; in all, the blazons illustrated on the amphora include an eagle, a bull, a tripod, a capricorn and a panther. (Archaeological Museum, Florence; author's photos, courtesy of the Museum)

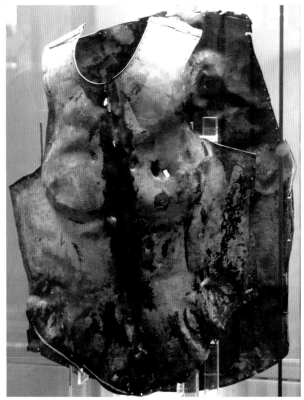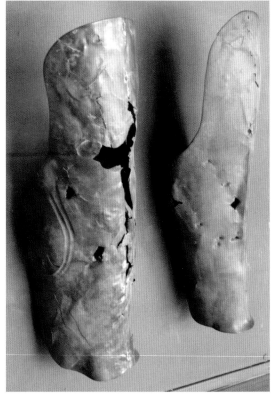

widespread use at a time when some groups in Central Italy were still using fire-hardened wooden spears.

According to Silius Italicus (VIII, 488), Vetulonia was the first Etruscan city to 'set battles ablaze with bronze'. Iconography, literary descriptions, and archaeology combine to create an image of wealthy warriors protected from head to foot with iron and bronze, and armed with spear, sword and shield. However, the material (such as it is) from funerary contexts reflects some profound differences between Northern and Southern Etruria, especially in the 7th to 5th centuries BC, as well as differences between cities within those broad regions. Differing resources in metal ore were one crucial factor. Indeed, we are told that in 507 BC a treaty exacted on Rome by Porsenna stipulated that the Romans should not use iron except for agricultural purposes.

OFFENSIVE WEAPONS

Swords and daggers

In the 7th to 6th centuries swords were an evolution of the Villanovan types, still very similar but now mainly in iron. From the 6th century Greek models were introduced alongside local ones, and these soon came to be preferred. The straight sword (*xiphos*) was that of the Greek hoplite, about 60cm (23.6in) long, but longer examples were also in use. Etruscan statuettes of this period usually show swords with straight, wide blades.

The curved sword (*kopis* or *machaira*), very popular in Greece and Spain, was, according to many authors, a Greek import from the East diffused in the Mediterranean area by mercenaries and merchants. However, Italian archaeologists believe that Etruscan swords of this typology were a local innovation developed from the curved Villanovan 'sabre'; they measured 60–70cm (23.6–27.6in) long, and were sharpened only on one edge. We have an early specimen dated to the 7th century, from Vetulonia, in which the swordsmith succeeded in creating a pattern-welded blade.

There is debate over whether we should look to Etruria for the ancestor of the Roman *gladius*, however much the Romans may have modified or developed it. Etruscan art shows almost every conceivable type of short, two-edged thrusting sword, but, beside the Greek imports, in the Orientalizing and Classical periods actual remains still show the persistence of the triangular shape, e.g. those discovered at Cerveteri, Corneto, Vetulonia and other places. The iconography points in the same direction: a pottery find from Clusium crudely represents warriors whose sword blades are triangular, with crescent-shaped pommels. Swords seen in the hands of two warriors on a golden *fibula* from the tomb of Pontesodo at Vulci (about 650 BC) are clearly thrusting weapons. The Tomb of Reliefs at Cerveteri, dating at the latest from the 4th to 3rd century, probably represents a period of transition from the triangular blade to that with parallel edges. About half of the specimens have triangular blades with just a suggestion of convexity, while the edges of the others are parallel for about two-thirds of their length, and then taper rapidly. These are good arguments for attributing to Etruria the introduction of the short cut-and-thrust sword as the origin of the *gladius*. A further shred of evidence is the Etruscan origin of the word *balteus*, 'baldric'. In the iconography the sword is usually represented as hanging from a baldric worn across the right shoulder. Several baldrics of dark brown or indigo leather are represented in the François Tomb, with scabbards presumably made of bronze-covered leather.

4th century BC Etruscan bronze panoply from the grave of the 'warrior of Settecamini' at Orvieto: breast and back plates of a *thorax statos* muscle cuirass, showing the heavily stylized musculature that was characteristic of Etruscan armourers; a heavy hoplite shield; greaves with muscled embossing; and a Montefortino-type helmet. (ex Golini)

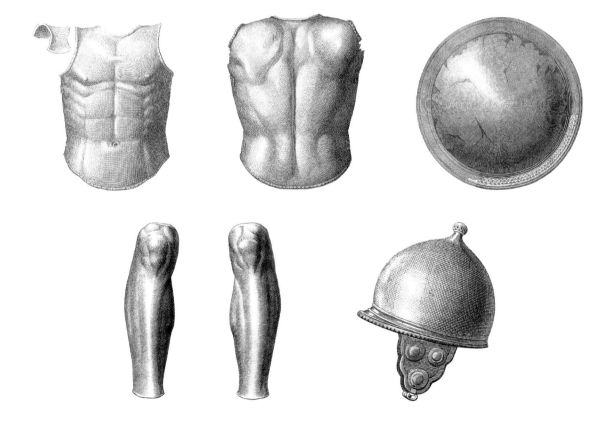

Some examples of high Etruscan metallurgy (e.g. from Clusium, 3rd century BC) have blades fashioned from alternating layers of harder and softer iron – a remarkable technical achievement for that period, showing an evolution of technique at the dawn of the Romano-Etruscan phase. Sometimes such blades were made from meteoric iron called *siderus*, which was considered to be of divine origin.

Axes

The axe was mainly replaced by the sword, but it was still a special feature in the Etruscan army. It was employed by infantry and some types of cavalry, and two-handed axes were used by distinct units. Its shape was derived from its Villanovan predecessor, but it was now made of iron rather than bronze.

Spears and javelins

Later Etruscan spears and javelins, in bronze as well as iron, are differentiated from Villanovan types mainly by longer heads. They maintained the triangular or leaf shape, and those made of iron sometimes did not need the reinforcement grooves. The fixing of the head to the wooden shaft was generally unchanged, but later specimens were perhaps forerunners of the Roman *pila*. A Romano-Etruscan *pilum* with an iron point 69cm (27in) long has been found in the 2nd–1st century BC Santuario dell'Acropoli in Volterra, and in the Giglioli tomb at Tarquinia three heavy *pila* are represented. The *pilum* from Volterra is clearly Roman, but it is noteworthy that this most traditional Roman javelin found its first iconographic representation on an Etruscan grave, and its prototype in the same grave. During the Punic Wars, Etruria was the arsenal of Rome: Populonia provided iron, and Arretium 30,000 shields and the same number of helmets, a total of some 50,000 *pila*, *gaesa* and *hastae*, and additionally miscellaneous metal items for 40 ships.

There is literary and archaeological evidence for crediting Etruria with the introduction of the *hasta* to the Roman Army. Pliny (VII, 201) records a possible Etruscan origin for the Roman *hasta velitaris*: '(invenisse dicunt) hastas velitares Tyrrenum'. Isidorus (*Orig.*, XVIII, 57) gives an alternative etymology, attributing its invention to the unknown town of *Veles*: 'Velites, from the Etruscan city called Veles'.

The thrusting spear was the main hoplite weapon, as attested by grave finds (Tomba dell'Orco) and iconography ('Amazons Sarcophagus'). A well-preserved painting on a terracotta slab of about 600 BC from Caere shows a highly developed Etruscan spear with its shaft in red and its metal point

THE LATE ETRUSCANS, 3rd CENTURY
(1) Rasenna mercenary, Tarchuna
An inscription from Tarquinia attests to the mercenary service of one of its townsmen at Capua during the Second Punic War. This warrior is copied from the so-called 'Amazons Sarcophagus' from Tarquinia, on which the decoration of each corselet is individualized, reflecting real-life practice. One of the major differences between Greek and Etruscan linen corselets in the monuments is that the latter are much more often decorated with painted floral and vegetal patterns.
(2) Rasenna marine, Roman fleet, Punic Wars
Etruscan marines served in the Roman fleet during the Punic Wars. The urns from Volterra which represent sailors or marines of the 3rd–1st centuries show the use of conical felt caps (*piloi*) and padded or quilted garments, probably made of felt and wool (*coactiles* and *centones*). The sea-fighters often employed axes (*secures*) and long, complex polearms (*drepana*) to cut the rigging of enemy ships when they came together for boarding actions.
(3) Aristocratic *eques* Marcnal Tetina; Clevsin, 225–200 BC
The last period of Etruscan armour-making shows the employment of composite armours with linen, padded and scale elements. Richly elaborated 'Hellenistic' helmets seem to be represented, worn by warriors on Etruscan urns from Volterra dated around 200 BC. These are often of the Phrygian shape, with a forward-curling extension of the dome, decorated cheek-guards, and two feather side-plumes.

in black. Further evidence for the development of spearheads is provided by some Etruscan spears preserved in Perugia, where two blades are arranged at right angles, thus giving four cutting edges, and at least one example presents three edges. The spear was mainly used for thrusting, but also, as represented in the Querciola grave (Tarquinia), to deflect other spears hurled at the warrior. For the 4th century we have from Montefiascone a single example of a pattern-welded spearhead of alternating soft and hard iron, but this highly advanced metallurgical technique was not widespread.

Bows, arrows and slings

In the 7th century BC the bow seems to have been part of the aristocratic warrior's equipment. On the Ischia of Castro wine-jug a fully armoured hoplite is seen bearing a bow, echoing the versatile fighting skills described by Homer. The Cannicella stele from Orvieto (end of 6th century) shows a similar depiction.

The aristocratic use of the bow was in opposition to the Greek hoplite ideal in that it depended upon individual expertise rather than esprit de corps, but archers are found in Archaic Etruscan art (e.g. the painted terracotta 'Campana slabs' contemporary to the Servian reforms, and the 'Boccanera' slabs, both from Caere). Etruscan graves from the Servian period in Latium have revealed more about archery. Finds of arrowheads are scarce, but 6th-century bronze examples have small angled wings, dovetail ends and conical or pyramidal sockets, while iron arrowheads have three wings. The empennage (fletching) appears in plaques as rather bulky. The points are either 'swallowtail' or leaf-shaped, both with cylindrical sockets. A rare example of a bronze arrowhead has been found in cremation-burial tomb 1 at Necropoli della Guerruccia, Volterra (first quarter of 7th century BC).

Rare traces of slings have survived from Etruria, and we know that the Etruscans stamped insults on their sling-bullets. An oval lead shot found in a deposit of slag at Populonia has the word *hur* incised, while others from different localities show *hurtu;* both words are clearly connected with the Latin *urtare* ('to wound'). An Etruscan slinger can be seen in the fresco in the 'Hunting and Fishing' tomb (Tarquinia): he wears a short tunic (or possibly a padded jacket and shorts) of light purple colour, and his sling has a red cord.

DEFENSIVE EQUIPMENT: HELMETS
Isidore (*Orig.*, XVIII, 14) tell us that the word *cassis* was Etruscan: '*cassidam autem a Tuscis nominatam: illi enim galeam cassim nominant, credo a capite* ('The Etruscans instead call the helmet *cassis*, I believe from "the head"'). The great variety of helmets found in different localities reveal that different

Front and back details of the mid-4th century BC bronze statuette known as the 'Mars of Todi'. In its design the armour resembles a *linothorax*, with conventional shoulder-guards fixed to bronze buttons, and worn over two superimposed ranges of hanging *pteryges*. However, it appears to be entirely covered with or reinforced by rectangular metal *lamellae*. (Etruscan Gregorian Museum, Vatican City; author's photos, courtesy of the Museum) types were in simultaneous use, even by hoplites of the same city. In the iconography the presence or absence of crests might represent differences of rank, but it is more likely that Etruscan elite warriors simply brought a wide range of equipment to the field.

'Pot' or 'bell'-shaped helmets

Less elaborate and diffused within Etruscan armies than in the Villanovan Period, the so-called 'bell'-type helmet had a one-piece bowl with a slightly flared lower border. Finds generally lack any decoration, and most would probably have belonged to the lower class of warriors. However, specimens highly decorated with geometrical patterns have been found outside the Etruscan areas (e.g. one from Tolentino). In Etruria the simple one-piece 'pot' is exemplified during the first half of the 7th century BC by the so-called 'Vetulonia' type (second circle of Pellicce and Tomba del Duce necropolis). These helmets were probably furnished with a leather chinstrap, and that found in the Tomba del Duce shows the remains of a probable bronze cheek-guard. The Vetulonia prototype, also visible on the Situla of Certosa, influenced Italic variants from which the Negau type derived.

Negau helmets

This was the most widespread typology (taking its name from a village near Zenjak, Slovenia, where a large number of these helmets were found). It typically had an egg-shaped form (e.g. Todi Museum), with a separate crest-fixing. Two sub-types were developed in the Etruscan world: the so-called 'Volterra' (third quarter of 6th century), and the 'Vetulonia' (predominant from last quarter of 6th century until 4th century). In a well-preserved bronze specimen of the Volterra sub-type (Staatliche Museen, Berlin, inv. L53) the helmet's dome is decorated with two lions and spiral motifs, and the frontal lower part with a small protruding lion's head. The Vetulonia typology shows small bosses located near the crown. This kind of helmet seems to have been cast as blanks and then worked into final shape by hammering.

Some examples are highly elaborated, like one from Pisa dated to the 5th century BC, which shows lateral spirals with flowers in the centre, a lion-shaped crest-holder and a frontal *protome*. Another, preserved in the Vatican Gregorian Museum, has cheek-guards shaped like a human beard, thus forming a sort of mask-helmet. Both these helmets are of Vulcian origin; Vulci was probably one of the centres of production for Negau helmets of the Vetulonia sub-type, and is also the source of separated elements

Painting of an Etruscan hoplite on the 4th-century 'Amazons Sarcophagus'; see Plate G1. The variations of decorative patterns seen in depictions of the linen cuirass argue that the artists had a detailed knowledge of changing fashions in such armours, which reflected an Italic tradition. (Archaeological Museum, Florence; author's photo, courtesy of the Museum)

Detail of an unarmoured hoplite from the 'Amazons Sarcophagus'; he wears a Phrygian style of the Chalcidian helmet and a blue *chiton*, and the artist emphasizes the arm-loop inside his shield. (Archaeological Museum, Florence; author's photo, courtesy of the Museum)

shaped like a Pegasus and Bellephoron, and prancing-horse protomes. Another beautiful specimen of Vetulonia type 2 (end of 6th–beginning of 5th century, from Caposcala), now displayed in the Vatican Gregorian Museum, is decorated in the frontal area with a small winged Silenus.

Negau helmets were widely dispersed in the Etruscan and Italic world (e.g. Arezzo, Fiesole). Evidence of their 'mass production' was the find at Vetulonia in 1905 of a deposit of no fewer than 125 examples inscribed with the clan name *haspnas*. These helmets would have been owned by the *haspnas gens* and distributed to their clients and vassals when necessity arose.

Corinthian helmets

The Corinthian-style helmet, well attested in Southern Etruria, was imported from Greece and used mainly by Etruscan hoplites. This helmet, with all its variants, is firmly attested in Etruria and Latium from the 7th century BC (e.g. finds at Vetulonia, Populonia and Civitavecchia). It offered complete protection to the head and face, covering the ears, cheeks, nose and neck while leaving the mouth and eyes exposed (at least in the specimens found in Central Italy). Particularly splendid examples are decorated with incisions (originally painted) or with applications of precious metal. Early Etruscan specimens were manufactured from hammered bronze sheet in two parts, but later examples were cast as blanks and then hammered. A Corinthian helmet dated 600 BC from Maremma (Tuscany) presents upper and back rings used to fix a crest-holder, probably made of wood.

Although some have suggested that such helmets were mainly ceremonial, they appear in battle scenes painted on some hundred Etruscan ceramic vessels. All but one of the warriors on the *oenochoe* from Ischia di Castro have Corinthian helmets, the exception wearing a Negau type. A vase in the shape of a Corinthian helmet from Tumulus III in Cerveteri (630 BC) is represented with a tall tube on the dome and a sphinx engraved high on the side.

Apulo-Corinthian helmets

From finds and artworks we know that the Etruscans, especially in the 5th and 4th centuries, used so-called 'Apulo-Corinthian' or 'Etrusco-Corinthian' helmets, a lighter version of the Corinthian type. This made its appearance on Attic vessels as early as the 6th–5th centuries throughout Central Italy, and is already depicted on figurines from Veii in the early 6th century (slab with departing warriors from the Piazza d'Armi sanctuary, Veii, Villa Giulia Museum). It was worn pushed up on the head rather than covering the face, as illustrated on the 'Amazons Sarcophagus' from Tarquinia (see page 4).

A splendid specimen from Vulci of type E under Bottini's classification (presenting the mask completely closed under the eyes and nose) is preserved at the British Museum. Its eye-sockets, brows and nasal piece appear as rather stylized. Sometimes a horizontal neck-guard was present, while the skull was often decorated with incised figures of boars. The fact that representations of Minerva in Latium and Etruria always show the goddess wearing such a helmet may link the use of it with the protection of that divinity.

Chalcidian helmets

The Greek Chalcidian type slowly replaced the Corinthian one, and it was widely used until the Roman period (e.g. pediment of Talamonaccio). Various specimens are preserved in Florence and Perugia Museums, although the most famous example was found at Todi in Umbria (5th century) – a highly decorated helmet with embossing on the cheek-guards and brow. Iconographic examples are the head of an Archaic bronze warrior from Volterra, a warrior figure on a terracotta *acroterium* from Falerii, and a statuette from Falterona. A young hoplite wearing a Chalcidian helmet decorated with a central crest and tall lateral plumes is represented in the Tomba delle Bighe, Tarquinia (490 BC), and a similar helmet in the closely contemporary Tomba della Scimmia, Chiusi (480 BC). Etruscan armourers from Vulci produced and used a rough variant of it, such specimens having a small neck protection and two round ear-guards decorated with spirals (Vatican Gregorian Museum).

Montefortino helmets

The famous Montefortino typology was a local Italic production probably of Celtic (Senones) origin. This helmet has been mostly found in Etruscan graves from the 4th century BC, like the Montepulciano example, or the beautiful specimen found together with bronze armour in a warrior tomb at Settecamini. It was in fact in that century that Etruscan workshops perfected their variants of such Gallic helmets, casting them by the lost-wax method.

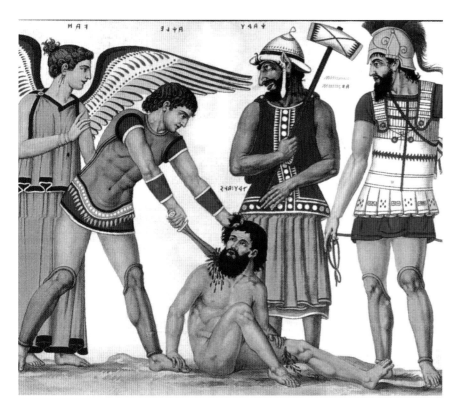

Detail from frescoes in the 4h-century 'François Tomb' from Vulci, copied by Ruspi from originals now in the Villa Torlonia, Rome. The scene is the Homeric episode when Achilles executed captured Trojans. Achilles (left) is depicted in a muscle cuirass, perhaps of leather. (Right) Ajax the Great – called Aivas Tlamunus by the Etruscans – wears a composite cuirass, apparently of linen with blueish-white coloured reinforcing *lamellae* on the shoulder-guards and chest. (Author's photo, courtesy of DAI Library, Rome)

A well preserved helmet from Umbria dated to the 4th–3rd centuries (Berlin Antikenmuseum, inv. L78) shows decorated cheek-guards and bronze applications of Celtic style.

This helmet is widely represented on ceramic vessels, in paintings and sculptures, and the 4th-century tomb reliefs at Cerveteri show them with scalloped cheek-guards. Actual examples (Orvieto) have been found with triple-disc cheek-guards, but by the 3rd century BC this typology seems to have been completely superseded by the long-lasting scalloped type, which was widely employed by the Roman army. Livy (XXVIII, 45,15) tells us that during the Second Punic War the Etruscan cities supplied men, weapons and equipment to the Romans, and that Arretium was a centre for production of helmets (probably of Montefortino type) and *pila*.

Hellenistic helmets

The so-called 'Thracian helmet', derived from the shape of Thracian and Phrygian caps, also came to Etruria. In some aspects it is similar to the Attic helmet, but it has a peak at the front which extends around the sides to protect both eyes and ears. It also has long decorated cheek-guards, usually cut away sharply at the eyes and mouth and curving outwards along the jaw. This type of helmet is worn by a hoplite painted on the 'Amazons Sarcophagus' and is also represented on the Giglioli tomb, both from Tarquinia and dated to the 4th century BC.

Due to the Hellenistic influence throughout Southern Italy, towards the middle of the 4th century the Phrygian helmet seems to have reached Etruria, with variants of Chalcidian and Conversano types. Among actual specimens the so-called 'helmet of Hannibal', produced in Southern Italy and actually belonging to a leader of the Tetina clan from Chiusi, is probably the best known. It corresponds with representations on sarcophagi of the 3rd–2nd centuries BC (Orvieto, Torre San Severo) and on urns (Turin).

Other helmets

A probable result of Venetic influence diffused among the Northern Etruscans is visible on the Situla of Certosa. This is a tronco-conical typology of helmets, similar to the famous example from Oppeano (Florence Archaeological Museum), which is formed from two sheets bent and riveted together to form a perfect cone. The same source shows another conical helmet with a long upper tube and reinforced with metal discs all around the bowl. Based on the specimen from Verucchio, grave 85 (last quarter of 7th century), this kind of helmet was probably made of a wicker frame with bronze elements attached.

The Pilos helmet, of Greek origin, was a conical type whose employment in the Late Etruscan period is attested by a cinerary urn ('Death of Troilus') from Volterra, and by the 'Amazon Sarcophagus' (Tarquinia). An actual 4th-century specimen is displayed in the Museo Gregoriano Etrusco.

Shields

The bronze-faced *aspis* of the Greek hoplite was in use among the Etruscans from the mid-7th century BC. Diodorus (XXIII, 2) tells us that 'At first [in ancient times] the Romans had rectangular shields for war, but later, when they saw that the Etruscans had [round] bronze shields, they copied them and thus conquered the Etruscans'. Bronze statuettes, pottery paintings, frescoes and urns often represent such shields, and actual specimens have been found.

In the cemeteries of the Osteria near Vulci a warrior's tomb (grave XLVII, 525–520 BC) contained a bronze helmet, greaves and shield. This included a pair of embossed plates, part of the shield's inner armbands, represented Achilles' ambush of Troilus at a fountain, and part of the shield's bronze facing. A bronze hoplite shield, together with bronze armour, comes from the warrior tomb at Settecamini, but the most complete example is the 5th or 4th-century shield from Bomarzo now in the Vatican Museum. This still shows remains of the wooden core, the leather lining, the bronze armband and the handgrip supports, and would have been lined with hide. Hoplite shields in the light Macedonian variant are visible in the hands of Late Etruscans in the Talamonaccio sculptures.

ETRUSCANS IN THE ROMAN ARMY, 2nd–1st CENTURIES BC

(1) Lictor
Painted urns from Volterra show *cornicines* and *lictores* attending victors or magistrates; this lictor is copied from the Tomba del Convegno (Monterozzi necropolis, Tarquinia). He is wearing the *toga gabina* and carries an iron double-axe (*bipennis*).

(2) Eques
An unusual urn from Volterra, representing the myth of Eteocles and Polynices, shows the brothers dressed like Roman cavalrymen of the period, with Boeotian helmets fitted with the *geminae pinnae* of Mars, shields of *popanum* typology, leather armour (*spolas*), greaves, and short swords.

(3) Centurio
This Roman centurion, copied from an urn in Florence Museum, wears a pseudo-Corinthian helmet fitted with a *crista transversa*. His composite armour is made of leather (shoulder-guards), padded material (main corselet), and on the chest bronze scales (*squamae*). Note his *calcei* boots, and the richly varied colours of his panoply.

(4) Guardsman
Reconstructed from the Sarteana urn, this Roman *miles* wears a late Montefortino helmet found in Forum Novum. His body armour combines a bronze *kardiophylax* breastplate and a *linothorax* corselet. We have added a single left greave and the curved oblong legionary *scutum* of his time; his weapons are the *hasta* and the deadly *gladius hispaniensis*.

(5) Magistrate
The absorption of Etruria into Rome saw leading Etruscan families climbing the government hierarchy. This official, copied from the famous statue of Aule Metele, wears the *toga exigua* over a *tunica*; the latter's purple *angusticlavi,* and the gold ring on his left hand, identify him as a member of the equestrian order. Hidden here, he would also be wearing high *calcei* boots with *lingula,* and fastened by *corrigiae*.

Detail of another Etruscan hoplite on the 4th-century 'Amazons Sarcophagus' from Tarquinia , this one wearing what is clearly a composite corselet of lamellar appearance. (Archaeological Museum, Florence; author's photo, courtesy of the Museum)

Oval or rectangular shields were also used, having variously-shaped central bosses. These *thureoi*, represented on the Situla of Certosa, show a rim, and a half-spherical boss upon which a small central protrusion is visible. A sharp-pointed type of boss is represented on a wall painting at Tarquinia, while actual bronze remains have been found in other places. Upon final-period oval or round shields (François Tomb; stucco of Tomb of Cerveteri reliefs) the boss was sometimes rendered as the head of a goddess, anticipating the decorated *umbones* of later Roman times.

The decorations on Etruscan shields have been little analyzed, but they included Medusa and lion heads. It is difficult to say if any of the emblems represent the *deigmaton* of a particular city or just the personal choice of the owner, but an indication of standardized emblems displayed by warriors of the same community is attested on a wine-jug from Tragliatella near Cerveteri (630–610 BC). The scene probably represents a departure for war; seven warriors, armed with three javelins each, carry large shields all decorated with a boar motif.

BODY ARMOUR & OTHER DEFENCES

Circular breastplates, like the one visible on a fresco from Cerveteri, developed from the earlier Villanovan pectorals. Although the triple-disc defence was probably never produced in Etruria, a Samnite example from Vulci, of probable Oscan origin, and other examples found in Etruscan graves, may confirm its use by the Etruscans as well (though Cowan does not exclude the possibility that these might be individual cases of war booty). Simple breastplates were used by low-ranking hoplites until the Roman conquest, and afterwards when Etruscans were incorporated in the Roman army.

Gualothorax and *statos*

The 'bell-cuirass' of Argos type was widely used by the first and second class of Etruscan warriors, as clearly attested by the iconography. These corselets reached just to the waist and had the lower edge rolled forward to catch downward blows at the groin or thighs, so are today called 'bell-shaped' or 'gutter-shaped'. A similar rolled edge protected the neck like a gorget. This armour appears in many pottery paintings, bronze figurines (e.g. warrior statuette from Ortona), *bucchero*-reliefs, and slabs (Tuscanella relief).

The early type of bell-shaped cuirass (γυαλοθωραξ) – almost smooth in appearance – was composed of a breast- and a back-plate fastened together with pins, rings and straps. Later variants, like those from Southern Etruria now in the Vatican Museum, show a fastening system comprising a full-length hinge complete with pin on the right side, and fastening buckles and straps on the left.

An evolved form – which appeared, rather tentatively, early in the 5th century, and became popular during the 4th – was the so-called 'muscle cuirass' (*thorax statos, stadion*). This was a bronze or leather corselet shaped in the form of a nude male torso. Again made in two pieces, it fastened at the shoulders and down the sides. Etruscans adopted it from the Italiote Greeks, but it was very soon adapted to local taste by the Etruscan armourers. Unlike earlier bronze corselets, which gave protection only down to the waist, most of these reach the iliac crest at the sides, while the lower borders curve down to give some protection to the lower abdomen at the front and the lower spine at the back. Unsurprisingly, none of the muscle cuirasses from Etruria have been found with shoulder-guards or a skirt of *pteryges*. These hanging protective strips were made of perishable material, and either attached directly to the rims of the armour or were parts of an organic under-armour garment.

A well-preserved muscle cuirass is among the bronze finds (second half of 4th century BC) from the Settecamini warrior tomb at Orvieto. Like other finds, including a contemporary armour from Vulci, it shows a feature that distinguishes Etruscan-made armours from Greek ones, namely an exaggerated and stylized musculature. The same is true of an armour of unknown provenance preserved in Karlsruhe, and of the armours from Bomarzo (one of which was intentionally destroyed for ritual reasons at the time of deposition).

Etruscan artists painted and carved scenes of men wearing the simple muscle cuirass. For instance, most of the various Etruscan versions of the scene of Achilles slaughtering Trojan prisoners at Patroclus's tomb show him wearing this armour while most of his followers wear a linen corselet. Details of the painting in the François Tomb strongly suggest that Achilles's armour is made of leather, but the same scene on the sarcophagus of Torre San Severo (Orvieto) seems to show the muscled armours of Achilles and Ajax Oileus as metallic. The war gear painted on the walls of the Tomba Giglioli (Tarquinia, end of 4th century) includes two fine muscle cuirasses, very like those on Apulian vases. Evidently, at that time the muscle cuirass was an expensive and prestigious possession.

At least two fragmentary terracotta figures from Etrurian temples represent men wearing the muscle cuirass, one from the Belvedere temple at Orvieto and the other from Roselle/*Rusellae*. The first shows neither shoulder-guards nor pteryges; the fragment from Roselle shows only the lower edge of the breastplate, but it too lacks pteryges. Both figures wear the cuirass over a full tunic whose skirt hangs in many vertical folds. Roncalli dates the Belvedere terracottas no

Etruscan-Umbrian bronze greaves, 350–325 BC, from burial chamber 25.05.1886, Frontone necropolis, Perugia. (National Archaeological Museum of Umbria, Perugia; author's photo, courtesy of the Museum)

Depiction of the monster Geryoneus in full composite armour, from the Tomba dell'Orco, 325-300 BC; watercolour by Jacobsen. (Author's photo, courtesy of the Library, National Archaeological Museum, Tarquinia)

later than the end of the 5th century BC; if true, this antedates almost all the preserved Southern Italian cuirasses, the Apulian vases and the Praenestine *cistae* representing them, as well as the Etruscan tomb paintings. In fact this handsome corselet looks very like the Apulian examples and the vase paintings they inspired.

Two interesting late 4th-century bronze statuettes wearing muscle cuirasses, from Verona (Archaeological Museum A4.95) and Vienna (Kunsthistorisches Museum AS VI 28), are believed to be of Etruscan origin. The first shows a high-necked cuirass without exaggerated musculature, the lower curve of both plates being rather shallow. The second statuette has a heavily-muscled breastplate, a relatively high, round neck, deeply cut armholes, and a rather short back-plate flaring over the buttocks; fastenings for the two plates are carefully reproduced under the arms.

Another bronze statuette in Florence (Archaeological Museum, 348) shows a tight muscled cuirass, presumably in leather; it has shoulder-guards cut from of the same piece of material as the back, and the neckline of the breastplate shows two little vertical wrinkles. Both plates are moulded like a metal cuirass, with the lower borders thickened and flaring.

Variants of Hellenistic armours with a short breastplate and pteryges, and often a sash knotted around the breast, are visible on urns and monuments from the 4th century up until the Roman conquest. The armours represented on the pediment of Talamonaccio (150–130 BC) show Etruscans already in the Roman army clad in what seems to be a leather variant, in one case decorated with a vegetal pattern on the breast.

Linothorax and composite armours

Just as the Corinthian helmet yielded to the more practical Chalcidian type, so the bronze 'bell cuirass' gave way to the lighter and more flexible linen corselet. This was made of layers of linen stitched or glued together, with shoulder-guards attached at the level of the shoulder blades and passed forward to fasten with cords to metal 'buttons' on the breast. Below the waist hung a double row of rectangular pteryges, the inner row slightly longer than the outer. The body might additionally be protected with metal plates or scales, either covering the whole or arranged in patterns. According to painters and sculptors, this corselet was usually worn over a short tunic which apparently opened down the front.

The many representations of the *linothorax* in Etruscan art indicate its wide range of diffusion, from the Archaic to the Hellenistic periods, and their quality reveals details of its composition. From the first half of the 5th century BC Etruria produced many bronze votive figures wearing such armours, and paintings also offer much evidence. Two of the most detailed depictions are visible on the François Tomb (Ajax Oileus) and the so-called 'Sarcophagus of the Priests' from Tarquinia. The best evidence of decorated and painted corselets come from the 'Amazons Sarcophagus', also from Tarquinia, dated to the second half of the 4th century BC; various *linothorakes* are shown, both simple or forming a sort of composite armours made of linen and leather and reinforced with scales. Other important sources are the painted architectural terracottas representing battle scenes or warriors (Caere, Civita Castellana, Orvieto, Falerii Veteres), and funerary urns.

Protective garments of composite construction are visible in Etruscan art from the 6th century, on bronze mirrors, urns, statuettes, sarcophagi, and especially in paintings. Scales covering the linen corselet are represented in a painting on the Tomba dei Vasi Dipinti (Tarquinia, 500 BC), and on a statuette from 475–450 BC (statuette of Laran, Florence Museum); these are similar to the Greek counterparts and are worn over a garment with a short double row of pteryges. Etruscan bronze figures showing similar armours come from the later 5th and the 4th centuries, the handsomest a figure from Falterona dated to 420–400 BC. The Tarquinia paintings reveal features identifying composite linen-and-plate cuirasses. In some cases the structure shows horizontal sections, consisting of rectangular (possibly reinforced) plates. The armour of Ajax Telamonius in the François Tomb (see page 49) shows horizontal bands with stitched connections, but the shoulder-guards and upper torso are protected by plates set vertically on the linen backing. Such plates are also represented in white, and traces of decoration in bright red may represent leather elements. A further type of composite cuirass, developed during the 3rd century and represented on funerary urns, were quilted linen *thorakes* with metal or leather scales covering the chest, back and shoulders. Often a semi-circular apron, rather like the old Greek *zosteres*, is shown covering the stomach, usually also plated with scales.

A 6th-century terracotta relief in the Louvre shows Etruscan warriors clad in leather armour. The stele of Avile Tites, from Volterra, shows the warrior armed with spear and axe, clad in a tunic beneath a *lorica* with shoulder-guards, proposed by Daremberg-Saglio, McCartney and Torelli to be an early representation of a leather *lorica*. According to Ducati, leather armour also seems to be worn on the Situla of Certosa, although of different lengths: extending only to the belt for cavalrymen, and to the groin for infantrymen.

Complete garments of ring-mail armour are visible on Etruscan warriors only from the 2nd century BC (frieze of Talamon), i.e. when they were under Roman rule.

Leg and arm protection

Greaves imitated Greek models, probably under the influence of the *Italiotai*. Local tastes are nevertheless evident in many actual specimens and on various monuments (e.g. sarcophagus from Torre San Severo). Made in copper alloy and put on by flexing the metal, the greaves feature the embossed muscles of the lower leg. The embossing was often artistically realized, as in an example decorated on the knees with embossed lion heads, sacred to Hercules (Villa Giulia Museum). Another pair of anatomic bronze greaves from Caposcala (end of 6th–beginning of 5th century BC, Museo Gregoriano Etrusco) show decorative engraved lines delineating the calves. In the late period greaves were left plain but were of no less beautiful craftsmanship, such as a pair surviving from the Settecamini tomb (second half of 4th century BC).

Interestingly, the Etruscans seems to have retained thigh protection later than the Greeks. This feature disappears from Greek panoplies at the beginning of the 5th century BC, but is visible in Etruscan iconography from the 6th at least until the 4th century (sarcophagus of Torre San Severo). The same is true for upper-arm defences; those in the François Tomb are represented in light blue, probably intended to represent iron or silvered bronze.

Some archaeological specimens of pieces of such armour retain fragments of lining in leather and sponge, to prevent chafing.

Cavalry and chariots

Some high-status bits with horse-shaped lateral elements in Volterra style come from graves VII and 58 of the Lippi necropolis at Verucchio (7th century BC), attesting to cavalry activity there. The Orientalizing Period saw the importation of swift and nimble breeds particularly suited for use as cavalry mounts.

Cavalry are often represented wearing Corinthian helmets. A 'horned' Corinthian-style helmet is worn by a horseman represented on a jar, probably from a tomb near Vulci (mid-6th century). It is possible that this depiction was modelled on a Southern Italian import of Greek provenance, like the specimens in the Staatiliche Museum Kassel, or found in Lucania and now in the local museum at Policoro (ancient *Heraclea*). Other helmets attested for cavalrymen are of Chalcidian typology, as painted in the Pulcinella Tomb (Tarquinia, 520 BC), showing a rider with a crested helmet and round shield.

The cavalrymen on terracotta reliefs are riding without any harness except for the bit and the reins. A very elegant harness of a Tarquinii cavalryman is represented in the Tomb of the Bulls; the horse presents a bridle with brown straps having a gold fitting at their intersection at the level of the ears. The bridle is decorated with hanging amulets, attached to a Thracian bit. The hooves and tail are painted blue.

As the *equites* entered battle as mounted hoplites, so the king of the 6th century took the field as a παραβάτγς. According to Helbig, a frieze slab

Coming under Greek influence from the mid-6th century onwards, the Etruscans depicted Greek mythological figures, but in the war gear of their own place and times. This detail from a carved Etruscan sarcophagus of the 3rd–2nd centuries depicts the popular myth of Eteocles and Polynices, the sons of Oedipus. Note the foreground figure's Phrygian helmet and composite armour, which includes a semi-circular 'apron', apparently covered with scales, protecting the abdomen. (Archaeological Museum, Florence; author's photo, courtesy of the Museum)

Detail from an Etruscan jar of *c*.550 BC, representing the myth of Achilles and Troilos. Here Achilles is depicted with a bronze panoply: a Corinthian helmet, with a crest showing tufts of three colours; an archaic Greek 'bell'-shaped cuirass; and anatomical greaves. (Photo courtesy of the Ure Museum, UK)

found at Toscanella represents the departure of an Etruscan army. A priest is followed by two hoplites and by a chariot, into which the heavily armoured king is stepping to take his place beside the driver. The remains of chariots have been found in graves of the 7th–6th centuries, suggesting that, in line with Eastern Mediterranean trends, there was an increasing use of war chariots, even more luxurious in appearance and faced with embossed sheets of bronze. In addition to transporting leading warriors, for whom they were status symbols, they proved an effective means of controlling outlying areas. A slab dated to the first half of the 6th century (Piazza d'Armi sanctuary, Veii) shows a one-horse chariot with fully armed warriors. From the second half of the 4th century, a four-horse chariot with eight-spoked wheels is represented on the 'Amazons Sarcophagus' from Tarquinia. Similar wheels are depicted up until the Roman period (e.g. Talamonaccio); in these later centuries chariots were probably used as a mark of prestige by magistrates, but no longer on the battlefield.

Rank symbols and insignia

The Etruscan kings' symbols of power were the golden crown, the purple tunic and cloak, the eagle sceptre, the ivory throne, and the *fasces*. According to Dionysius of Halicarnassus (II, 29) and Livy (II, 8) these were the first royal *regalia* that the Etruscan kings introduced into Rome.

Dionysius (III, 61-62) mentions that Tarquinius Priscus carried a gold and ivory *sceptrum* decorated with the golden eagle of Jupiter. His assertion is confirmed by Virgil (*Aen.*, VIII, 506) and Silius Italicus (X, 41), according to whom the word *sceptrum* was of Etruscan origin. The latter author also states that *fasces* – the axe bundled with rods, symbolizing the power to beat

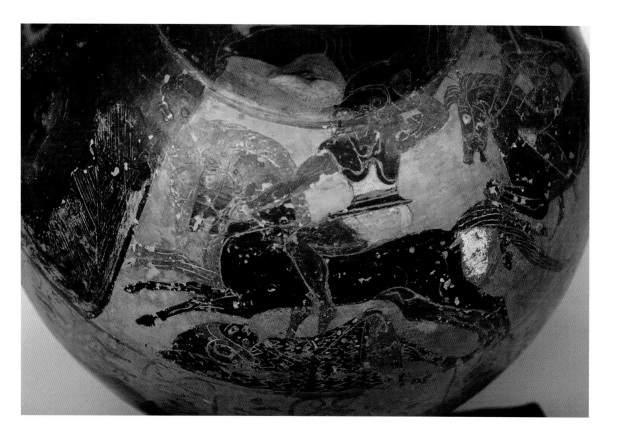

and to execute – originated from the city of Vetulonia (VIII, 483–485), from which an interesting specimen survives. The François Tomb is the earliest source (portrait of Vel Satie, owner of the tomb) of the *toga picta*, a garment embroidered or painted (the Latin *picta* had both meanings) with naked warriors and scrolls on the borders, which was worn by kings in triumphal processions. According to Dionysius, Florus and Macrobius, Tarquinius Superbus also had such a gold-embroidered purple toga (*Rom. Ant.* III, 61; *Epit.* I, 5; *Sat.* I, 6, 5).

On the other side of the jar is a horseman; he has a horned Corinthian helmet, and an unusual – composite? – bell-cuirass lacquered in two different colours and fitted with shoulder-guards. (Photo courtesy of the Ure Museum, UK)

On 6th-century BC *stelae* Etruscan princes are often represented holding a spear and an axe as symbols of royal power, the former anticipating the *hasta summa imperii* of Roman times. Etruscan generals held the double-axe, symbolizing (like the fasces) their *imperium*: the power of life and death over their men. It is enough here to recall the axe found in Vetulonia, and the funerary stele of Auvele Feluskés from nearby Castiglione della Pescaia (7th century BC), on which the warrior prince is brandishing the double-axe.

As for *signa* in the Roman sense of unit standards, the sources support the thesis that the Etruscans had animal standards, which the Romans imitated. Roman sources (Lydus, *Mag.* I, 8; Serv., *Aen.* XI, 970) also attributed to the Etruscans or to the Sabines the origin of the *signa manipularia* – tactical standards used to locate the command centre of troops in battle.

Musical instruments
Most of the main musical instruments played by the Roman army in the Consular and Imperial periods were of Etruscan origin, and musicians are well attested in Etruscan military iconography. The trumpet, together with

the shield and the axe, appears as a symbol of the military authority of a Tarquinian prince as early as the first half of the 7th century BC.

An Etruscan origin is attributed for the *tuba*, the instrument played by the *subulo* (*tibicine, tubicen*; Varro, *De Lingua Latina*, VII, 35; Festus, 403). According to one tradition it was widely used among the Tyrrheni, being invented by their eponymous forefather Tyrrhenus himself. Other Roman sources report that the Etruscan kings Piseo (founder of Pisa; Plin., *Nat. Hist.* VII, 56) or Maleus of Regisvilla or Vetulonia (Lact., *Comm. In Stat. Theb.* IV, 224, VI 404) were the first to adopt the trumpet to transmit orders to troops fighting in close formation. Likewise, the Greek tragedians refer to trumpets as 'Tuscan'.

Athenaeus (IV, 82, 184) states clearly that κέρατα (horns) and trumpets were both Etruscan inventions. Amongst the first instruments for religious and military use was the *lituus*, a type of tuba with a curved

Painted terracotta plaque from Caere, 600–550 BC; British Museum. This shows conclusive evidence for the use of animal standards by the Etruscans; note the central figure's staff surmounted by a bull emblem. (ex. Murray, 1889)

end (Livy, I, 78). An intact specimen from Caere, 1.6m (5ft 3in) long, is now in the Vatican Gregorian Museum. Its military use is attested by Etruscan paintings and terracotta reliefs (e.g. slab from Cisterna di Latina, Ashmolean Museum, Oxford). Again, the Romans inherited the *lituus* from the Etruscans, preserving its shape, and using the term *tuba tyrrena* to differentiate it from their long, straight trumpet. According to Diodorus (V, 40, 1) the Etruscans also found the *salpinx* (a trumpet resembling but shorter than the tuba) useful for military purposes, and used it when working out infantry tactics.

Clothing

We know from vase paintings and bronzes (Verona, and Vienna statuettes) that the cuirass was usually, but not always, worn over a short, loose tunic. This is usually visible at the throat, the upper arms, and as a short, full skirt which often left the genitals partly exposed. This is not surprising, given that many warriors fought naked, or only covered by armour reaching the waist. Sometimes (Firenze statuette) the tunic presents a short, full skirt in narrow vertical folds and no sleeves. Red-coloured tunics were characteristic, and still used by Late Etruscans in the Roman army (Talamonaccio sculptures, urns).

An Etruscan fashion introduced from the 6th century BC was a sort of jacket covering the breast (stele of Larth Ninie from Fiesole, last decades of 6th century). This was often replaced with the short Greek tunic reaching the upper thighs, so often visible under hoplite armour. The colours visible in Etruscan paintings are white, black, red, purple, sand, ochre, brown, green, and light blue. The Sperandio Sarcophagus (early 5th century) shows warriors armed with spears returning from battle. Their military outfits are carried on pack mules, while they wear long calf-length tunics and *tebenna* cloaks, some of them fitted with hoods.

From the 6th century onwards Etruscan elites made widespread use of calf-length boots with flat or raised points (Sperandio Sarcophagus). For wealthy officers we may also suppose embroidered leather shoes reinforced with bronze. Warriors also sometimes wore bronze-reinforced wooden sandals, but often they went barefoot. Importantly, among the iconography we also find early representations of the famous Roman *caligae*, which were probably of Etruscan origin (urns from Volterra and Perugia), including details of the nailed soles (frieze from Talamon).

SELECT BIBLIOGRAPHY

For reasons of space, we can list here only the ancient sources and the most relevant modern works. A much fuller Bibliography of academic publications can be found on the Osprey website by following: www. ospreypublishing.com/eli_223_bibliography.

ANCIENT SOURCES

Athenaeus, *The Deipnosophistae*, Gulick C. B., 7 vols (Loeb Classical Library, Harvard University Press, 1927–41)

Callimachus, *Hymns and Epigrams, Licophron, Aratus*, by Mair, A.W. & G.R. Mair (Loeb Classical Library; London, 1921)

Diodorus Siculus, *Bibliotheca historica*, Vols I-V (eds) Imm. Bekker, L. Dindorf, Rec F. Vogel (Lipsiae; Teubner, 1883–1906)

Dionysius of Halicarnassus, *Roman Antiquities – Rhomaike Archaiologia (Rom.)* (Loeb Classical Library; Harvard UP, 1913–37)

Herodotus, *Le Storie* [*History*], (eds) A. Colonna & F. Bevilacqua, Utet SpA, Turin (1996)

Festus, Sexti Pompei, *Festi De verborum significatione quae supersunt cum Pauli Epitome,* (ed) Muller, K.O. (Leipzig, 1880 (1839); Hildesheim, Olms, 1975)

Florus, L. Annaeus, *Epitome of Roman History* (trans) Forster, E.S. (London; Harvard UP, 1928)

Granii Liciniani reliquiae, (ed) Criniti, N. (Leipzig; Teubner, 1981)

Isidorus, Isidori Hispanensis Episcopi Etymologiarum sive Originum Libri XX, ed. Lindsay W.M., vol. I-II, Oxford, 1911.

Ineditum Vaticanum, by H. von Arnim (ed.), Hermes, 27. Bd., H. 1 (1892), 118-130

Lactantius, Placidus, *Commentarii in Statii Thebaida, et Commentarius in Achilleida,* Vol 1, Statius, Publius Papinius, *Opera* (Teubner, 1898)

Lydus, *Mag. – Ioannis Lydi, De Magistratibus Populi Romani Libri Tres,* (ed) Wunsch, R. (Lipsiae, 1903)

Livy, *History of Rome from the Founding of the City – Ab Urbe Condita* (Loeb Classical Library; Harvard UP,1924-49)

Macrobius, *Saturnalia* (Columbia University Press, 1969)

Maurus Servius Honoratus, *Commentarii on the Aeneid of Vergil,* (ed) Thilo, G. (Leipzig, 1881)

M.Verrii Flaccii, *Fragmenta, Post Editionem Augustiniana denuo collecta atques digesta, Sexti Pompei Sexti fragmentum, ad fides Ursiniani exemplari recensitum,* (ed) Eggers, A.E. (Paris, 1839)

Plin. HN. – Plinius, C. Secundus (Maior), *Natural History,* 10 vols, (trans) Rackham, H. (Cambridge, Mass; London, 1969–79)

Propertius, *Elegiae – The Elegies,* (ed) Goold, G.P.(Loeb Classical Library, Harvard UP; 1990)

Silius Italicus, *Punica,* 2 vols, (trans) Duff, J.D. (Cambridge, Mass; London; Harvard UP, 1983–89)

Strabo, *Geographica – Geography ,* II, Books 3-5, (trans) Jones, H.L. (Loeb Classical Library, Harvard UP; 1923)

The Fragments of the Roman Historians, Vol I, Introduction, (ed) Cornell, T.J. (Oxford, 2013)

Varro, M. Terentii, *Varronis de lingua latina librorum quae supersunt* (Leipzig, 1833)

Virgilius, P., *Vergilii Maronis Opera omnia,* Pts I-III, (ed) Forgiger, A. (Lipsiae; Teubner, 1873–75)

MODERN WORKS

Babbi A. & Peltz, U., *La tomba del guerriero di Tarquinia,* Romisch-Germanisches Monographien. Bd. 109 (Mainz, 2013)

Bentini L., Boiardi, A., von Eles, P., Poli, P. & Rodriguez, E., *Il Potere e la Morte. Aristocrazia, guerrieri e simboli* (Verucchio, 2006)

Bietti-Sestieri, A.M. & E. Macnamara, *Prehistoric Metal Artefacts from Italy (3500–720 BC) in the British Museum* (London, 2008)

Bottini, A., Egg, M., Von Hase. F.W., Pflug H., Schaaff, U., Schauer, P. & Waurick, G., *Antike Helme: Sammlung Lipperheide und andere Bestände des Antikenmuseums Berlin.* (Mainz; Verlag des Römisch-Germanischennak Zentralmuseum, Mainz, 1988)

Cateni, G. (ed.), *Etruschi di Volterra* (Cenate Sotto, 2007)

Cherici, A., 'Armati e tombe con armi nella società dell'Etruria Padana: analisi di alcuni monumenti' in *La colonizzazione Etrusca in Italia, Atti del XV convegno internazionale di Studi sulla Storia e l'Archeologia dell'Etruria, in Annali della Fondazione per il Museo 'Claudio Faina',* Vol. XV (Orvieto, 2008) pp.187–246

Connolly, P., *Greece and Rome at War* (London; 1988 & 2006)

Cowan, R., 'The Art of the Etruscan Armourer', in Turfa, M. J. (ed), *The Etruscan World* (London & New York, 2013) pp.747–758

De Marinis, G., 'Pettorali metallici a scopo difensivo nel villanoviano recente' in *Atti e Memorie dell'Accademia La Colombaria, XLI* (Florence, 1976) pp. 1–30

Emiliozzi, A. (ed), *Carri da Guerra e principi Etruschi, catalogo della mostra* (Rome, 2000)

Fossati, I. , *Etruscan Armies* (Milan, 1987)

George, D.B., 'Technology, ideology, warfare and the Etruscans before the Roman conquest' in *The Etruscan World* (London & New York, 2013) pp. 542-549

Gleba, M., 'Linen-clad Etruscan Warriors', in Nosch, M.L., *Wearing the cloak: Dressing the Soldier in Roman Times* (Oxford & Oakville, 2012) pp. 45-55

Hencken, H., *The Earliest European Helmets, Bronze Age and early Iron Age* (Harvard UP, 1971)

Kilian, K., 'Das Kriegergrab von Tarquinia' in *JdI* (1977, 92) pp. 24–98.

Martinelli, M., *La lancia, la spada ed il cavallo, il fenomeno guerra nell'Etruria e nell'Italia centrale tra età del bronzo ed età del ferro* (Florence, 2004)

Marzatico, F. & Gleischer, P. (eds), *Guerrieri, Principi ed eroi, fra il Danubio ed il Po dalla Preistoria all'alto Medioevo* (Trento, 2004)

McCartney, E., 'The military indebtedness of Early Rome to Etruria', in *Memoirs of the American Academy in Rome,* Vol I (Bergamo, 1917) pp.122-167

Menichelli, S., Magno F., & Orsingher, G.P. ,*Etruschi guerrieri* (Viterbo, 2008)

Pericoli, U. & Conde, R., *Las Legiones Romanas* (Barcelona, 1976)

Pflug, H., *Schutz und Zier, Antiken Museum Basel + Sammlung Ludwig* (Basle, 1989)

Cyegelman, M. & Rafanelli, S. (eds), *Io sono di Raku Kakanas, Vetulonia: la tomba del duce* (Vetulonia, 2004)

Richardson, E. H., 'The Muscle Cuirass in Etruria and Southern Italy: Votive Bronzes', in *American Journal of Archaeology,* Vol. 100, No. 1 (Jan., 1996) pp. 91-120

Sannibale. M. *Le armi della collezione Gorga al Museo Nazionale Romano* (Rome, 1998)

Saulnier, C., *L'armée et la guerre dans le monde etrusco-romain, VIII-IV siècles* (Paris, 1980)

Sekunda N., & Northwood. S., *Early Roman Armies* (London, 1995)

Talocchini, A., 'Le armi di Vetulonia e Populonia', in *Studi Etruschi,* XVI (1942)

The Axel Guttmann Collection of Ancient Arms and Armour, Part 1 (London; Christies auction catalogue, 2002)

The Axel Guttmann Collection of Ancient Arms and Armour, Part 2 (London; Christies auction catalogue, 2004)

Tomedi, G., *Italische Panzerplatten und Panzerscheiben* (Stuttgart, 2000)

Torelli, M. (ed.)., *Gli Etruschi* (Cinisello Balsamo, 2000)

INDEX

Figures in **bold** refer to illustrations.